Contents

CD 2

Introduction

Overview

World Sound Matters is a fully-integrated anthology of music from around the world, consisting of:

❐ 2 compact discs of 58 traditional music recordings, representing 35 different countries
❐ notated transcriptions of each recorded example
❐ explanatory texts covering the special context of each style and its musical content
❐ 2 sets of progressive pupil listening-based questions for each musical style

Each unit is free-standing and can be effectively used on its own. Alternatively, multiple units can be combined, in any order, to provide an introduction to the musical traditions of the world.

The music incorporated in *World Sound Matters* has been carefully selected and prepared by an ethnomusicologist in consultation with other music specialists and professionals actively engaged in music education. Two aims have been paramount: on the one hand, readers need analyses of a wide range of musical traditions which are both authoritative and yet remain accessible to the non-specialist; on the other hand, the many musicians whose work appears on the sound recordings deserve a thorough and sympathetic study which neither cheapens nor dilutes their artistry.

The result is a publication which should be of practical use to a wide range of musicians, from secondary school teachers to their pupils, from adults interested in knowing more about world music to music students wishing to specialize in this field, and to composers.

Studying the Music of the World

Why is it important to understand something of the music of the world? Why should we not remain satisfied with our own musical traditions, whether popular, classical or something else? Various reasons have been proposed. For some, the pay-off lies in the fact that greater familiarity with musical styles simply expands the amount of music one can appreciate and thereby derive pleasure from. For others, the study of unfamiliar music brings to mind aspects of our own music-making which we habitually disregard. The greater sensitivity to music which results encourages a deeper engagement with and re-evaluation of our favourite kinds. A third view is that developing an understanding of foreign music is a significant part of the broader educational process of learning to respect human cultural diversity.

There is surely value to each of these proposals, yet I would like to add one more to the list: we need to study music because it is a very special part of human life. All around the world, music affects individuals in ways we barely understand. Music helps people project an identity; it assists them in the recollection of the past and in their prayers for the future. It offers a channel of expressive communication and a vital outlet for human creativity. If we are to understand fully what it means to be human, we need to discover how and why music operates in the ways it does. To expect to accomplish this from examining only the evidence of a single musical tradition, even one as rich and well-documented as that of Western art music, is surely unrealistic. Instead, just as botanists look at plants from around the entire globe or historians study the rich and poor of all nations, we need to consider the whole world's music.

Yet it hardly needs to be said that if world music is to receive a larger share of a school's music curriculum, the music teacher will need to be convinced that it offers an efficient means of imparting musical skills and experience, as compared to more familiar musical forms. After all, when dealing with deeply familiar music, an experienced teacher can more easily design a lesson and turn unexpected questions in profitable ways. Also, given that resources for investment in new materials and the time to master their use is typically scarcer than teachers might wish, the teacher may feel more confident setting out along well-furrowed paths. The question remains, then, that even if one accepts that there are good reasons for expanding the focus of music education to include music from all around the earth, is it actually practical to do so, bearing in mind the input of time and resources this will necessitate?

The issue of practicality has guided the compilation of *World Sound Matters*. There would be little point in offering teachers written material that did not dovetail with the associated sound recordings, or of including sample pupil questions which cannot be readily answered by the teacher with reference to the sound recordings, transcriptions or written notes. Also, there seemed little to gain from producing a text which attempted to cover the whole world. Such an anthology would likely be of immense size, or would have to skate over the surface of what was important in each individual musical tradition. Instead, a range of interesting traditions, with a considerable geographical spread, was selected for deeper investigation. In many cases, two or three examples from the same country or region are presented, reinforcing the point that not all music from each of these places will sound the same, and allowing scope for regional project work. Although the ordering of the material suggests that a geographical approach is to be taken, the possibilities for cross-cultural comparison are extensive. These opportunities are mentioned both in the accompanying notes and the pupil questions; use of these will allow teachers to readily link examples from different cultures to create a coherent world music course.

Those are the guiding principles behind this publication. It is now worth briefly describing each part of the set, how it was assembled and ways in which it might be used. Naturally, teachers will be likely to think of their own means of employing this material too.

1. The CDs

These contain a series of music tracks, ordered just as in the accompanying books. Each track is licensed from a commercially available CD, since I wanted further sound material to be readily accessible to those who were attracted to these extracts. Nonetheless, the tracks in themselves are extensive enough to give a good idea of the musical style in question, and often contain complete songs or pieces. Many are live performances, recorded 'in the field', and include the sounds of the community at large as well as the musicians themselves. We are perhaps more accustomed to listening to cleaned-up, studio recordings, and may find disconcerting the occasional bark from a Balinese dog, but these tracks communicate a real sense of arising from actual social events.

The availability of suitable sound recordings from which tracks could be licensed naturally influenced the eventual content of the anthology as a whole. Some exciting musical traditions had to be omitted because of the difficulties of locating a suitable recording. Others would have required a longer extract than could have been accommodated, and occasionally I thought it preferable to omit a musical tradition altogether rather than give it too little space to justify itself properly.

Apart from their use in class to illustrate lessons derived from the accompanying texts, or by pupils working through the sets of questions, the CDs can easily be used as revision aids. By playing back tracks previously studied and asking leading questions, the teacher – armed with the transcription and accompanying notes – can readily test pupil knowledge and aural ability.

2. The Transcriptions

The hardest task in the compilation of this anthology has been the production of the book of notated transcriptions. Ethnomusicologists such as myself are trained to write down musical sound in visual symbols, but we rely on contextual knowledge of the music as much as on our ears. Knowing how an instrument works, how its strings are tuned, what its performance techniques are and what the local music theory admits as acceptable greatly assists the process of converting musical sounds to graphic signs. However, this familiarity is not easily acquired, and there are probably few ethnomusicologists with intimate knowledge of more than three or four different musical traditions. Sometimes, specialists in the music of other cultures helped by contributing transcriptions and notes, and a handful of my bolder students at the University of Durham gave of their best efforts. Nonetheless, it was not always possible to find someone with both the requisite local knowledge and the free time to undertake each transcription, and most of them I completed myself. The further I moved from familiar territory, which in my case means Chinese traditional music and Western classical music, the harder it was to find ways to write down what I thought I heard.

The phrase 'thought I heard' is important, because the human ear and mind are closely linked. Hearing music is not a passive process of taking in sound waves. It involves perception, or the making sense of the sounds, which is where experience and training come in. This means that a transcriber has no choice but to rationalize each set of sounds to his or her own ways of thinking about music. I may have detected patterns where the originators of the music would say that none exist, and I may have thought I heard intervals or rhythms which are not quite those so carefully performed by the musicians. Of course, I have very probably made straightforward errors too, but the point of explaining all this is to stress that musical perception is quite an individual quality and one greatly reliant upon a listener's experience. Given this variable, written transcriptions of musical sounds, however accurate, will never be able to tell the whole story. The sound recordings should, of course, be taken as authoritative, and the transcriptions as subsequent attempts to describe them in writing. They are thus quite unlike the scores of Western musical works, where the symbols typically prescribe a series of notes which, when realized adequately by the performer, should result in the sounds the composer had in mind.

Despite all this, written transcriptions are extremely convenient tools, allowing the viewer to take in a whole piece in one glance, or to compare, outside of the passage of performance time, different passages. In general, the transcriptions in this collection employ stave notation. Stave notation has the advantages of being both widely understood and a very condensed means of writing down certain musical information. It is strong on pitch and rhythm, which are graphically laid out on the vertical and horizontal axes respectively. It is less strong on attributes such as timbre or microtonal adjustment of existing notes, aspects which are very important in some musical traditions. For reasons such as these, the stave notation employed is typically adapted in some way, for instance an adjusted key signature or layout, to better suit the facts of the music in question. Special symbols are explained in each case, and additional comments to guide the viewer are found on every transcription.

The transcriptions are designed primarily for use with the sound recordings. A few, especially the unaccompanied songs, are suitable without further adaptation for use as performance scores. Even in these cases, though, I would still recommend learning the songs by ear from the recording and using the transcription as a supplementary guide.

Another role of the transcriptions might be to act as models for pupils' own project work. In many music curricula it is possible for a pupil to complete a special extended study. Partial transcriptions could be continued by students equipped with the original CD. Or, taking the transcription and its accompanying notes as a model, they could perhaps study an alternative track from the same recording.

A further possible use of these transcriptions is as a resource for composers. By this I mean not so much imitating the sounds of different musical traditions, although one could perhaps have fun doing that. Instead, close study of the ways in which different people from around the world combine musical sounds and structure musical passages will suggest musical techniques to those who are interested in structuring sounds in their own musical idioms. For reasons of focus, this line of thought is not pursued much further in this anthology, but the imaginative reader will find much scope here for fruitful experimentation.

3. The Teacher's Manual

The explanatory texts which accompany each musical example and transcription are grouped in a separate book. In most cases, the intention has been to discuss the cultural background of the specific recording, to give pertinent details to the genre in question, to describe the main instruments or techniques employed and to provide a musical analysis of the actual excerpt itself. Illustrations and supplementary musical examples or charts are frequently incorporated. Material has been drawn from specialist ethnomusicological studies and reference works in various languages as well as interviews with an international team of ethnomusicological experts and traditional music performers. Sometimes, I have used part of the space available to introduce a broader social, cultural or psychological issue suggested by the music. Sections of this kind should be useful in encouraging cross-cultural comparison, or, in other words, stepping back momentarily from the individual details of a specific example to consider larger musical trends and problems. Although much of the other information needs relatively little processing before it is suitable for pupil consumption, these theoretical sections are perhaps better thought of as being for teachers themselves than as something for them to break down and pass on. Still, with intelligent groups of older pupils it might be possible to use some of these ideas directly also.

Following on from the last point, provision of specific sample lesson plans has been avoided. Different teachers will want to use this material in different ways according to the age, size and aptitude of the class they are faced with. Although lesson outlines could have been prepared, and one suggestion is made in the next section, it seemed better to leave the specifics of delivery to the teachers concerned.

Apart from the manual's use as a source of lesson material, the explanatory texts could perhaps be given, in whole or part, to advanced pupils to work through on their own with reference to the sound recordings and transcriptions. These notes could form the starting points of more extended, independent studies of a particular music culture, style or instrument.

4. Pupil Question Book

This part of the anthology consists of two sets of sample pupil questions, one set designed to be answered whilst listening to the excerpt, the other intended to be worked subsequently with reference to the transcription. Not all of the questions are of the type that might be set in public examinations, and a few will require many repetitions of the recorded performances, and perhaps some class discussion. Questions vary from the factual and straightforward to the more open, interpretative type, but, in the main, they have the function of pointing out features of the music. Some require written answers, others selection of the most probable of several alternatives, and still others reflection upon the techniques through which answers are achieved. Inclusion of this last kind of question acknowledges that the development of problem-solving skills in musical listening may eventually be of greater utility than the memorization of any amount of repertory. A primary thrust of an effective music education must be to equip pupils with the skills to deal with whatever musical experiences they encounter during their lives.

Earlier, I mentioned that one of the aims of *World Sound Matters* was not to provide sample lesson plans. This is true, but it does occur to me that in certain cases it might be possible to use the two sets of pupil questions supplied for each track as the backbone of a classroom lesson. Instead of simply posing each question, the teacher could perhaps ask a series of leading questions which draw the pupils toward each point raised in the written questions.

The above remarks have been directed primarily at music teachers and, by reduction, their pupils, but there are others who might find *World Sound Matters* useful. For instance, beginning students in the subject of ethnomusicology might well find the recordings, transcriptions and explanatory notes helpful as a basic survey of world music. Those who teach world music surveys at universities and colleges may find the recordings, transcriptions and notes helpful. Some of the pupil questions remain worthwhile at tertiary level also.

Likewise, for trainee-teachers and their instructors, this publication provides both a considerable amount of material for classroom use and also a practical example of how the theoretical concerns of a subject as seemingly inconsequent as ethnomusicology can be made relevant to larger audiences.

Final Remarks

There are so many peoples and cultures around the world that there is constant pressure to compress the mass of available information into digestible chunks. Only partial introductions to each musical style can be provided, and, in the hope of depicting the remarkable international variety of human music-making, the examples chosen are often among the most idiosyncratic from a particular area or people. Throughout the anthology, because of the necessity to condense information, there is a general non-emphasis on the individuals involved in each recorded musical event. These people, whether composers, performers or listeners, are important and deserve respect and recognition. When reading the notes on a particular people in this book, try to imagine what would have to be left out from a similar-length passage on the music of your own people. When listening to the recorded examples, even when two or three are provided for a country, decide which two or three examples you would choose for your home nation, and whether everyone in your country would agree with your choice. Certainly, I am sure that many people from around the world would not have chosen the extracts I did to represent their musical practices.

There are many sources of information available to those interested in world music. Specialist books on individual countries or traditions are not mentioned here, but amongst those concerned with world music in general some of the most widely accessible are:

1. Reference Works

The New Grove Dictionary of Music and Musicians, ed. Stanley Sadie. London: Macmillan (1980). The twenty-volume *New Grove* contains an enormous amount of information on music of the world. Generally, this is organized into entries for each country or region, but some important instruments and genres have their own entries. Most entries in *New Grove* also contain useful bibliographical lists. A revised edition, which should be even more up-to-date, is currently in preparation, as is a several-volume encyclopedia of world music from Garland in New York.

The New Grove Dictionary of Musical Instruments, ed. Stanley Sadie. London: Macmillan (1984). This three-volume dictionary is the best source for further detail on musical instruments from all around the world. Even when an instrument has a special entry in the original *New Grove*, it was often expanded or updated in this dictionary. Photographs and diagrams are common. Spelling of instrument names in this anthology follows that used in the *New Grove Dictionary of Musical Instruments*.

Microsoft's CD-ROM *Musical Instruments* (1994) contains a wide selection of traditional instruments from around the world. Attractively illustrated and with sound extracts available at the click of an icon, this kind of resource provides a very effective means of exploring the world's musical traditions. In the field of music education, the possibilities of multimedia are extensive and exciting, and will probably prove more influential than in subjects where sound serves only an illustrative purpose.

2. World Music Surveys

Music Cultures of the Pacific, the Near East, and Asia, 2nd ed., William P. Malm. Englewood Cliffs: Prentice Hall (1977), and *Folk and Traditional Music of the Western Continents*, 3rd ed., Bruno Nettl. Englewood Cliffs: Prentice Hall (1990). Originally prepared in the 1960s, these two surveys remain useful today. Clearly written and authoritative, they discuss main musical styles, instruments and compositions. Illustrations and sample transcriptions are frequent.

Worlds of Music: An Introduction to the Music of the World's Peoples, 2nd ed., gen. ed. Jeff Todd Titon. New York: Schirmer (1990). This valuable book from a team of ethnomusicologists examines several musical cultures, and communicates the processes through which world musics may be investigated. A sound recording is also provided.

Excursions in World Music, Bruno Nettl et al. Englewood Cliffs: Prentice Hall (1992). With its own cassette, this attractive book introduces several representative world musics, including that of the Western art tradition. No sample lessons are offered in this publication, but there is much clear discussion of key musical and cultural aspects, bibliographies of further sources and lists of sound recordings.

Multicultural Perspectives in Music Education, ed. William M. Anderson and Patricia Shehan Campbell. Reston, Virginia: Music Educators National Conference (1989). Team-written by both educators and ethnomusicologists, this very useful volume introduces the music of many parts of the globe, providing short notations as part of sample lessons.

Lessons from the World: A Cross-Cultural Guide to Music Teaching and Learning, Patricia Shehan Campbell. New York: Schirmer (1991). This thought-provoking book examines and compares music learning from around the historical and contemporary world. Implications for present-day teachers are drawn and sample applications provided.

3. Journals

Much new research on world musics appears first in specialist journals. Perhaps because ethnomusicologists know that the majority of their readers will not have first-hand experience of the music they are dealing with, their writing is often accessible to the intelligent but non-specialist reader. Individual teachers who require a regular flow of information on world musics may wish to subscribe to an ethnomusicological journal or investigate whether it is possible for them to consult these in their local university libraries. Many university libraries allow visitors to consult their books and journals; at some, for an annual fee equivalent to the price of a single text book, it is possible to borrow materials.

Among the several journals specializing in this subject, the foremost is *Ethnomusicology*, currently published by the Society for Ethnomusicology at the University of Illinois. Issued three times a year, *Ethnomusicology* contains articles, book reviews, film and recording reviews and geographically-ordered lists of new publications. The latter are very useful for tracking down the latest information on specific musical traditions. For more applied information, frequently embracing traditional musical styles, teachers might find useful the *International Journal of Music Education* published by the International Society for Music Education at the University of Reading.

Credits

Japan – Music for *Shakuhachi*	transcription & notes	Ruth Lenihan
Korea – Music for *Kŏmun'go*	transcription & notes	Robert Provine
Laos – Music for *Khāēn*	transcription & notes	Katy Grainger
Indonesia – Javanese *Gamelan*	transcription	Simon Steptoe
Indonesia – Balinese *Gamelan*	transcription & notes	Laura Doggett
Australia – Aboriginal Music	transcription & notes	Harriet Gaywood
Ethiopia – Song with *Masenqo*	transcription & notes	Paul Hayday
Russia – Play Song	transcription & notes	Marzanna Paplawska
Romania – Professional Folk Music	transcription & notes	Helen Roome & Ellen Scott
Romania – Music for *Cimpoi*	transcription & notes	Helen Roome & Ellen Scott
Trinidad – Music for Steel Band	transcription & notes	David Price
Brazil – Ritual Dance-Song	transcription & notes	Catherine Bancroft

Acknowledgements

Dorothy Almond, Merete Anderssen, Ron Berry, Ross Blyth, Peter Burt, Hilary Chung, Minh Chung, Catherine Crichton, Katherine Davies, Kevin Dawe, Keith Getty, David Greer, Jonathan Haig, Grammenos Halkias, Adam Holladay, Ronak Hussein, Roman Ivanovitch, Yoshikazu Iwamoto, Natsuko Kato, John Koegel, Peter Nickol, Peter Owens, Dimitra Stamogiannou, Joo-Lee Stock, Charlie Stokes & Susie Winkworth

facing page: **World Map showing where the music in this anthology originated**

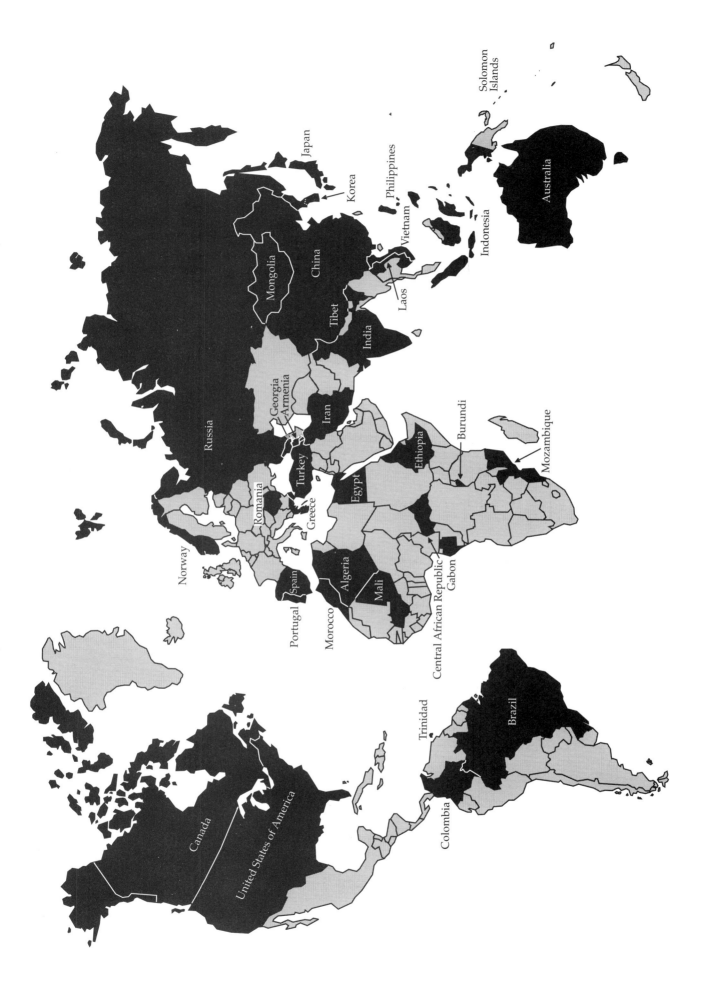

Gagaku Court Music

Cultural background

Gagaku, music of the Japanese court, is a particularly interesting musical tradition with a performing history of many centuries. Much of this music was originally imported from neighbouring countries, including Korea and China. The Chinese also collected foreign music like this, and some of the pieces transmitted from ancient China to Japan were originally from Central Asia, for instance the piece *Etenraku* discussed below. *Gagaku* pieces were carefully maintained by hereditary imperial musicians, and some present-day Japanese musicians claim that this music sounds just as it did one thousand years ago in China. However, from early music notations and other written evidence we can tell that over the centuries a number of changes have taken place.

Instrumentation

The instruments used in *Etenraku* include winds, percussion and strings. The wind and string instruments play in a heterophonic style, i.e. each musician performs the tune simultaneously, but with differences appropriate to the capabilities and characteristics of the instrument. Percussion instruments mark the beats with a series of rhythmic patterns. Most of the instruments used in *gagaku* music were first brought to Japan over a thousand years ago, along with the compositions.

The instruments used in the modern *gagaku* ensemble are: the mouth organ *shō*, bamboo flute *ryūteki*, cylindrical double-reed pipe *hichiriki*, small gong *shōko*, small drum *keko*, large drum *taiko*, thirteen-stringed zither *sō* (also called the *koto*) and four-stringed lute *biwa*. Although the music can be played with one instrumentalist to each part, performances with multiple wind and string players to each part are also found. There is no record of the *hichiriki* in the oldest surviving historical sources, so this instrument appears to be a more recent addition. However, its strong, penetrating sound makes it a dominant instrument in the *gagaku* ensemble, and many Japanese hear the *hichiriki* and *ryūteki* as principal melodic instruments, the others providing harmonic and rhythmic support.

Notation

Amongst the oldest *gagaku* notation are tablatures for the lute *biwa*. These tablatures assign a symbol to each open string and fret. The *biwa* had four strings, each with four frets, so, including open strings, the player needed to learn twenty main symbols. There were also secondary symbols which show metrical structure, rhythmic subdivisions, repetitions and so on. These symbols were written in columns read from top to bottom beginning on the right-hand side of the page.

Japanese music uses a similar series of twelve semitones to the West. In an old *biwa* tutor book, instructions on how to tune the strings are given, and by following these instructions (and assuming that each note is the same duration) we can convert *biwa* tablature into staff notation.

 Track 1

Structure

Etenraku

Etenraku was originally a very short piece – basically with three phrases, each played twice:

Etenraku, from *biwa* notation, with ornaments omitted

Its structure can be represented like this:

AA BB CC

Sometimes the opening section was repeated again at the end. The extract notated in the Transcription Book and recorded on the CD is the first section and its repeat: **AA**.

Gradually, over the centuries, short pieces like *Etenraku* have been expanded, in two main ways:

a) The melody has become stretched out, with extra notes added between and together with the melody notes.

b) The structure has become more complex. Today, a tuning-up passage (**I**) is often played as an introduction to *Etenraku*, phrases **A** and **B** are repeated after phrase **C**, and a coda (**D**) is added. Nowadays a full rendition of *Etenraku* will probably follow one of these plans:

I AA BB CC AB D or
I AA BB CC AA BB D

The stretching-out of the melody is so extreme that the original melody is difficult to hear – and indeed is unknown to many modern performers. Each note of the twelfth-century tune has become a four-beat bar of music, and each eight-beat phrase has become an eight-bar section. By comparing the first note of each bar in the transcription with the first phrase of the music above, we can discover the original tune. The only exception is bar 6 where the *ryūteki* flute player performs an F instead of the G in the old tune, but even here, on the repeat (bar 14), the *biwa* player supplies the G.

To see the way additional notes have been inserted, look at the *biwa* part in bar 9. What was once a single note (d) – the first note of the repeat of phrase **A** – has become a spread chord (E–B–e–d). Similar expansion is found when old and recent parts for other instruments are studied. In the mouth organ *shō* each note of the simple melody has had cluster chords of several different pitches added to it. The *ryūteki*, on the other hand, can produce only one note at once, so it ornaments the original tune with a wide variety of melodic decorations, variations in breath pressure and so forth.

Music for *Shakuhachi*

Cultural background

In Japan, the vertical flute is thought to have been brought from China in the eighth century. Once there, it passed through various transformations, emerging in the seventeenth century as the *shakuhachi*, played by a Zen Buddhist sect of ex-samurai, beggar-priests called *komuso*, 'monks of the void'. For these monks, playing the *shakuhachi* was a form of meditation as well as a means of requesting alms. Gradually the instrument was adopted by lay musicians as well, and today there are several styles, or schools, of performance, amongst which the Kinko and Tozan schools are the most prominent.

The *shakuhachi*

The *shakuhachi* is an end-blown flute with a notched blowing edge and slightly curving, flared end. Made of thick bamboo, it has four finger-holes on the front and a thumb-hole behind. The word *shakuhachi* describes the length of the instrument, *shaku* meaning 'one foot' and *hachi* 'eight', i.e. 1.8 feet. Today, many different-sized instruments are used, although the 1.8 *shaku* model, approximately 55cm long, is considered standard.

The standard *shakuhachi* gives a basic scale of d', f', g', a' and c". Nonetheless, accomplished musicians can produce other pitches, including semitones and microtonal inflections, over a range of three octaves. A variety of techniques are used for this. For instance, by lowering the head slightly so that the air enters the instrument at a different angle the pitch drops by a semitone or a tone. In general, these notes sound more softly than those blown regularly. Other head movements and breathing techniques are used to manipulate tone colour, vibrato and microtonal decoration. The tongue is little used in *shakuhachi* performance; when repeated notes are required, finger movement is generally used to articulate repeated pitches. However, flutter-tonguing is sometimes employed.

Notation

As with many other Japanese instrumental traditions, *shakuhachi* music has its own notation, which varies slightly according to the school of performance. Typically notation comprises adapted Japanese *katakana* phonetic symbols arranged in vertical columns, starting on the right-hand side of the page. Smaller symbols indicate register, ornamentation, repeated notes and the use of certain breathing techniques or head movements. Rhythmic values can be shown by dashes, and by scoring vertical lines through or beside the pitch symbols (similar to the tails given to staff notation quavers and semiquavers). Otherwise, duration can also be approximately indicated through the relative length of a line connecting one pitch symbol to the next. Most dynamic and articulatory techniques are memorized by the player. Thus, although students learn from scores, they also pay close attention to the interpretation their teacher demonstrates.

***Shakuhachi* music**

Shakuhachi music is divided into two main categories: *honkyoku*, 'original pieces', and *gaikyoku*, 'foreign pieces'. As far as musicians from the Kinko school are concerned, most of the thirty-six *honkyoku* were collected in the eighteenth century by the *komuso* Kurosawa Kinko (1710–71), establisher of the Kinko style of performance. The majority of these pieces are meditative in character and have descriptive or evocative titles. Various styles of portamento and microtonal adjustment are important to this music. The music in the *honkyoku* repertory is very strictly fixed; no improvisation is permitted on the part of the performer.

Gaikyoku pieces are both more numerous than *honkyoku* pieces, and more regular in terms of metrical structure. The *gaikyoku* category is subdivided into three broad types of music: *sankyoku* 'trios' (also played solo) for *shakuhachi* with *koto* zither, *shamisen* long-necked lute and voice, in which the *shakuhachi* might imitate the sounds of the stringed instruments; *minyo* 'folk songs', played either solo or to accompany a singer; and *shinkyoku* 'new pieces', predominantly twentieth-century works by Japanese and Western composers, some in an international avant-garde style.

Track 2

Kokū

Kokū ('Empty Sky'), a piece from the *honkyoku* repertory, concerns a tale of the mystic monk Fuke in ninth-century China, renowned for ringing a handbell whilst advising onlookers of certain esoteric phrases. Having realized that death was imminent, Fuke asked an obliging passer-by to nail the lid down on his coffin, Fuke having already lain within. Hearing of this, people rushed to the site but, opening the lid, found the coffin empty and the sound of a handbell ringing ever fainter in the sky.

In keeping with the mood of this piece, the recorded performance employs a larger *shakuhachi* than usual, pitched a third lower. Many of the phrases consist of long notes which, after being articulated and decorated, gradually die away. In this, we perhaps detect the influence of the meditative style of performance preferred by the early *komuso*.

The beginning of the composition is shown in the transcription. The music is through-composed, but certain phrases or short patterns are re-used throughout; compare, for instance, phrases 2 (bars 5–10) and 7 (bars 35–39). Numerous finger, head and breath techniques are illustrated in this piece, for example the employment in bar 24 of an accent involving breath hissing audibly across the blowing edge. Note also the extremely subtle control of dynamic levels, a feature shown less satisfactorily in staff notation.

Music for *Kōmun'go*

Cultural background

Korea has often been characterized as a cultural bridgehead reaching out from China towards Japan. It is true that the Koreans adopted many aspects of historical Chinese language and culture, including some musical instruments, and were at certain times politically and economically dominated by either China or Japan, but we should not underestimate the contribution of native Koreans to their traditional musical forms. Although a Korean instrument or ballad-singing style might have been inspired by those of Chinese traders, or a Korean court musical repertory reconstructed from imperial Chinese manuscripts, the Koreans necessarily did so in light of their own previous musical experiences. For instance, when an instrument was imported it might be adapted to fit local tuning preferences and performance techniques, reconstructed from indigenous materials and brought into existing musical genres.

South Korea is also important in the contemporary world as an economic and technological power. Under considerable pressure to modernize during the past century, and particularly since 1945, the Koreans have been forced to re-evaluate their most traditional forms of cultural expression, deciding what role is appropriate for them in a modern nation-state. Initially, the traditional arts declined as influential people dropped them to embrace those of the West, which they perceived as being more modern and international. Recently, however, growing economic and political self-confidence, and demonstration of the Korean ability to master Western art forms, has led to a resurgence of interest in what makes Koreans special as themselves, i.e. their traditional culture.

The Korean government has looked for various ways in which to preserve and promote these traditional forms, such as the establishment of university music departments and schools which train students in the performance of traditional instruments. One method is particularly interesting. This is the designation of carefully selected musicians (and other artists) as 'intangible cultural assets'. On condition that they continue to perform and teach their specialism, these individuals are given state grants and considerable status. Yet, Korean musical traditions are actually being transformed quite radically by these attempts to preserve them. Older, regional styles are giving way to many performers imitating a single, national style (that belonging to whoever is chosen as a living cultural treasure). Also, a concert-style setting has become typical for musical genres that might once have been performed for personal pleasure.

The *kōmun'go*

The *kōmun'go* is a form of fretted zither with six silk strings, distantly related to such instruments as the Chinese *qin* and Vietnamese *dan tranh* (see China: Music for *Qin*, and Vietnam: Music for *Dan Tranh*). The strings are sounded with a stick-like bamboo plectrum, which is struck against a leather covering on the body of the instrument for emphasis. Two strings are used to play the melody, while others are plucked in ornamental patterns. The left hand stops the strings near one of the frets, commonly pushing the string laterally to adjust its tension, thereby altering the pitch. Performers recognize quite a number of different pushing techniques and positions, and can produce a passage of several different notes by manipulating the string once it has been plucked. Vibrato is performed by rapidly moving the string back and forth, while a common decoration is to sound a note with the string tension a little too high and then immediately drop down to the correct pitch.

For several centuries, the *kŏmun'go* was prominent as a court instrument in Korea, occurring in various elite ensembles and as a solo instrument. Towards the end of the nineteenth century, however, the musician Paek Nakchun had the idea of playing folk-style *sanjo* music on the *kŏmun'go*, a trend which proved popular.

Sanjo

Sanjo is a genre of solo instrumental music which arose during the latter part of the nineteenth century from various modal, melodic and rhythmic elements common to most forms of south-west Korean folk music. Performed at first on the *kayagŭm* zither, it was then adopted by the players of other melodic instruments, such as the *kŏmun'go*. The originators of this style apparently improvised melodies based on traditional modal patterns, but subsequent generations have tended to memorize the models developed by their teachers. A traditional performance passes through a series of different metres, which are mapped onto a progression from slow to fast tempo. Typically, a *sanjo* performance begins with slow 18/8 time and leads through moderate 12/4 and swinging 12/8 metre to end with fast music in 12/8 and 6/4.

Whatever the solo instrument, a *changgo* hourglass drum provides a rhythmic accompaniment. One end of the drum is struck with the hand while the other is sounded with a slim stick. The drummer, whose part is not as fixed as that of the soloist, emphasizes the main beats of the metre and may link the soloist's phrases with more continuous patterns. Use of characteristic rhythmic patterns helps to create the required mood of each metre.

 Track 3

Sanjo for *kŏmun'go* in *kyemyŏnjo* mode

The transcription is an excerpt from the second section of a *sanjo* performance, that in 12/4 metre, or *chungmori*. The tempo is moderate, and the drummer emphasizes beat 1 and particularly beat 9 of each twelve-beat unit. (A 'half-bar' mark is provided on the transcription after beat 6 for orientation). The drummer also fairly consistently employs rhythmic patterns such as the lightly-played double grace note and pair of quavers found in the middle and at the end of each bar.

The melody of the music is derived from the *kyemyŏnjo* mode central to the music of south-west Korea. In this mode there are three important pitches or pitch areas: tonic (C in the transcription – a semitone above recorded pitch), dominant (G, played with much vibrato) and supertonic (which can range from D through Eb and E to approximately F). Other notes (mostly Bb, A and F) appear for decorative purposes. Both the dominant and supertonic carry the expectation that the tune will resolve to the tonic, although resolution can be temporarily delayed. Most melodic phrases last six beats and end on either the tonic or dominant. The excerpt shows a gradual fall in register (bars 1–4) followed by a rise across the whole range of the *kŏmun'go* (bars 5–12).

Music for *Qin*

Cultural background

One of the oldest Chinese musical traditions is that of the seven-stringed zither *qin* (pronounced 'chin'). This was the instrument of the Confucian scholars who administered the Chinese empire for two thousand years until the twentieth century. These men (only men could become officials) were musical amateurs, playing the *qin* for pleasure. Apart from music, they studied calligraphy, painting, poetry, philosophy and literature. When they performed, it was not in public concerts but for a few friends. Sometimes, they played for themselves, either alone at night or at an attractive beauty spot. Pieces were usually performed solo, although duets with the voice or the vertical flute *xiao* (pronounced 'she-ow') were also popular. This music was preserved in a complex form of tablature, described below.

Some *qin* players believed their music was too subtle for common ears and would be corrupted by the presence of 'barbarians' (i.e. most foreigners), women, tradesmen and the uneducated. In fact, there are several well-known female *qin* performers in Chinese history, and a number of foreigners have learnt the instrument. Today, the *qin* is taught in Chinese music conservatories, and played in formal public recitals as well as at private gatherings.

The *qin*

The *qin* has seven strings, traditionally silk but now often nylon. The strings stretch over the wooden body of the instrument, pass over a bridge and through holes in the body to tuning pegs underneath. The *qin* body is hollow, to increase resonance, and is made of well-seasoned wood coated with dark varnish. Along its length are thirteen inlaid studs to show the player where to stop the strings.

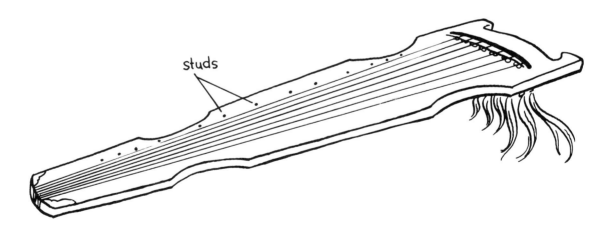

studs

The *Qin*

Tuning and mode

Various string tunings are used in *qin* music, but the most usual is this pentatonic scale: C, D, F, G, A, c, d. Theoretically, any of these could be treated as the fundamental of a mode and used for cadences. In the piece *Meihua san nong* (see below) most sections begin and end with F.

Notation and technique

Qin tablature combines symbols from written Chinese, telling the performer which string to pluck, how to pluck it, where to stop the string, which stopping technique to use and what ornamentation to add. This example combines four Chinese characters:

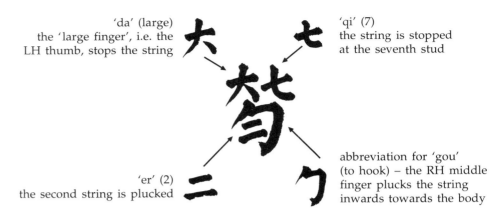

'da' (large)
the 'large finger', i.e. the LH thumb, stops the string

'qi' (7)
the string is stopped at the seventh stud

'er' (2)
the second string is plucked

abbreviation for 'gou' (to hook) – the RH middle finger plucks the string inwards towards the body

A Typical Symbol from *Qin* Notation

Usually, the second string is tuned to D below the bass clef. Stopped at the seventh stud, exactly halfway along the string, and then plucked, a note one octave higher results. The same note can also be produced with different plucking techniques and on the other strings. All would have different sonorities, and all would be notated with different symbols.

Rhythmic values are not indicated in this tablature. *Qin* players used scores to learn the technique required for a new piece or to revise an old one. Generally they studied with a teacher or friend, who could remind them of the rhythm. As soon as possible, the score was put aside and the player performed from memory. Also, *qin* players wanted their music to have a meditative character, and believed every performer should develop personal interpretations of the rhythm of each piece.

Qin notation was written in vertical columns read from right to left across the page. Today, it is commonly written in horizontal rows, a result of Western influence on Chinese writing habits. Some modern *qin* scores publish *qin* notation and staff notation versions of the same tune together, the *qin* symbols underneath the staff symbols to which they correspond.

Right-hand performance techniques include plucking inward or outward with each finger and the thumb, as well as strumming several strings with one finger, running several fingers over one string, and plucking two strings together. Left-hand techniques include simple string-stopping, slides (before, during or after a note), and many different styles of vibrato. Sometimes, the left thumb plucks the strings as well. Harmonics are performed by stopping the strings lightly with the left hand, and (unlike fully stopped notes) cannot be ornamented by slides or vibrato.

Qin music

More than three thousand pieces for *qin* have been preserved in scores, although the majority are no longer performed. Most are descriptive, with programmes suggesting a musical picture or short story. Musical structure is often sectional, with music from earlier passages brought back and reworked in later ones. It is particularly common to hear harmonics in the introductory and coda sections of long pieces, but they may also be used in the middle, as in the solo *Meihua san nong*.

 Track 4

Meihua san nong

The title of this composition, 'Three Variations on Plum Blossom', refers to a flower the Chinese associate with elegance, purity and strength. In winter, when the blossom appears, it was traditional to display a bough in the home. 'Three Variations' describes a theme played three times in this piece. This is one of the best known Chinese *qin* pieces, and is quite old, its score dating from 1425. Nonetheless, since every player is expected to develop a new interpretation, every performance combines old and new.

Meihua san nong has ten sections and a short coda (sections 6–9 are shown on the transcription). Section 1 is a slow, low-register introduction. Sections 2, 4 and 6 are three variations of the Plum Blossom theme. The other sections all present contrasting themes in different registers of the instrument, although material is shared between sections 5 and 8 and between 7 and 9. The composition is further unified by the use of the same codetta phrase (see bars 135–141) in several sections.

Transposition is used to give variety to repeated material. For example, although sections 7 and 9 are related, much of section 9 is an octave lower than section 7. This gives it a contrasting sound while still allowing the listener to notice resemblance between the two passages. Rhythmic and melodic development also add variety; for instance, compare bars 129–130 with 131–132.

Jiangnan *Sizhu* Ensemble Music

Cultural background

Jiangnan *sizhu* is a genre of instrumental ensemble music from the villages and towns of the Jiangnan in east China. *Sizhu* ('silk and bamboo') refers to the silk-stringed bowed and plucked instruments and bamboo-tubed wind instruments which predominate in this music. Traditional *sizhu* is amateur music performed from memory by groups of friends in tea shops. It used also to be played at public occasions such as weddings, where it would accompany the procession of a bride to her new home and the feasts which follow. In the tea shops, listeners are welcome to enjoy the music, but it is not performed for them so much as for the performers themselves. Other musicians waiting their turn sit nearby and sip tea, smoke or chat, as in the recorded extract.

Style, instrumentation and texture

Group co-operation is more important than individual virtuosity in *sizhu* music since the musicians simultaneously play personal versions of the same basic melody. Players respond to one another during performance, interweaving patterns of ornamentation and imitating melodic patterns. This informality extends to instrumentation, which can vary quite considerably from one occasion or piece to another. A typical group, however, includes one or two players of the two-stringed fiddle *erhu*, four-stringed lute *pipa*, three-stringed lute *sanxian*, hammered dulcimer *yangqin*, bamboo transverse flute *dizi* (or vertical flute *xiao* in soft pieces), mouth organ *sheng* and, the only exception to the 'silk and bamboo' name, a pair of wood clappers or a wood block.

During performance the percussionist gives a clear beat, sometimes enlivening it with a few syncopations. The other players all perform heterophonically; that is, each recreates the same tune in an attractive and new manner, usually adapting it to suit better the characteristics of his own instrument. (Almost invariably 'his', not 'her'.) No two performances should be identical, and *sizhu* musicians listen carefully to each other to discover new variations for the melody. There is no leader, but the *dizi* has a loud sound and is easy to gesture with, so performers often follow the *dizi* player, especially when beginning, ending or changing tempo.

Mode

Jiangnan *sizhu* music is largely, though not exclusively, pentatonic. That is to say that the great majority of the notes in the basic tunes are from one or another pentatonic scale – some tunes modulate from one pentatonic mode to another. However, two additional pitches per octave are quite often used in ornamental patterns, which converts the five-note pentatonic scale to its heptatonic (seven-note) form. In the piece transcribed, *Huanle ge*, the principal notes are D, E, F♯, A and B, of which D is the final, while G and C♯ are the two extra notes, generally restricted to decorative use:

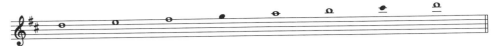

Pentatonic Scale with Ornamental Heptatonic Notes (in black)

Metre and ornamentation

Jiangnan *sizhu* music, like much other Chinese music, uses a range of metres. There are slow tunes, with four or eight beats to the equivalent of a bar, moderate tunes with two or four beats per bar and fast tunes with one or two beats per bar. Several of the melodies in the *sizhu* repertory are played successively in slow, moderate and fast versions.

The music analyst can divide Jiangnan *sizhu* ornamentation into: 1) fingered grace notes, mordents, trills, slides or tremoli (depending on the instrument) – added when convenient and attractive to a melody at any speed; 2) melodic passing notes, escape notes, auxiliary notes, reiterations, etc. – inserted between the basic notes of a melody. At a slow tempo there is time to add more of the second type of decorations, so slow-metre tunes are much more ornate than their faster relatives.

Passing notes are like those in Western music, except that Chinese musicians choose their passing note from either pentatonic or heptatonic forms of the same scale. The escape note is similar: it ornaments a step by leaping just beyond the notes of the step itself. Auxiliary notes decorate a repeated note by moving up or down a step.

Passing notes		Escape notes		Auxiliary note
pentatonic passing note	heptatonic passing note	lower escape note	upper escape note	lower auxiliary note

Typical Ornaments in Jiangnan *Sizhu* Music

 Track 5

Huanle ge

This piece, 'Song of Happiness', is one of the eight main pieces of the Jiangnan *sizhu* repertory. On the recorded performance an ensemble of *dizi, erhu, sanxian, yangqin, pipa* and wood block is used. The tune is played three times, once at a slow speed with much ornamentation, once at a moderate speed with a little less decoration and finally very quickly indeed, though still with some grace notes, trills and other ornamental pitches. The opening of each rendition is transcribed. Although *Huanle ge* sounds through-composed, some passages are repeated. However, because different decorations are used each time, it is difficult for the non-performer to spot repeats, except perhaps in the final, fast-metre rendition.

Chuanju Opera

Cultural background

Chinese traditional opera exists in a great variety of regional and local styles, experts counting around 350 different types. Some are no longer performed, some are recent creations and others have histories of several centuries. The majority mix speech, song and instrumental passages to tell historical or mytho-logical stories with elaborate costumes, actions and facial make-up. Props and scenery are generally few, and the same basic tunes are re-used in different operas of the same style.

To make each opera interesting, singers adapted the basic tunes in performance to make them fit the specific words and character portrayed. Skilled performers could produce new stories swiftly, improvising scenes or adapting them from other operas. Many opera troupes travelled around performing at theatres, temples, tea houses and markets; the more stories available at short notice, the more time for profitable performance and the less for unpaid rehearsal or travel.

Role types

Most traditional Chinese opera relies upon a number of standard role types, each with a set style of acting, singing, costume and make-up. Accustomed listeners can recognize a melody as being that of, say, a young scholar role. From the appearance of a character, audiences have a good idea about his or her age, social background and personality.

The principal role types are the *sheng*, *dan*, *jing* and *chou*. Male *sheng* are subdivided by age, and whether the character is an acrobatic military type (for whom singing is less important) or a civilian Emperor, scholar (often the male lead in romances) or courtier. Female *dan* are similar, common roles being the demure young mistress (the female lead in romances) and her flirtatious maid-servant. Both *sheng* and *dan* have fairly restrained make-up. *Jing* are usually military, and have brightly-painted faces and flowing beards. The colours and patterns are symbolic – for instance white portrays treachery and red loyalty. *Chou* are normally lower-class, crafty or comic characters: perhaps servants, inn-keepers or thieves. They have white make-up around the nose, and speak a more rustic variety of Chinese than the others, sometimes cracking improvised jokes.

Staging conventions

In traditional performances, a table and pair of chairs are arranged in conventional patterns which audiences recognize as, say, a court-house, tavern or mountain pass. Smaller props are also found, for instance the use of a whip to symbolize a horse. The colour of the tassels represents the horse's hair, and from the way the whip is held, viewers know whether the actor is mounted or leading the horse. In contemporary performances and films, more lavish scenery is often used.

Sichuan opera

The recorded performance illustrates the regional style *chuanju* from Sichuan, West China, which has a history of three centuries. Many operas in this style have an unusual characteristic: the use of a small supporting chorus to comment on the actions of the principal characters or repeat their lines (most singing in present-day Chinese traditional opera is solo). Other special features of *chuanju* are the dance-like movements of the characters on stage, and the importance of percussion instruments in the accompaniment. As well as wooden clappers and a variety of drums, the percussionists play a wide selection of gongs and cymbals. To mark the start or end of certain scenes a *suona* oboe is also played.

 Track 6

The Legend of White Snake

This tragedy concerns the White Snake spirit, which through years of self-cultivation has acquired magical powers and the ability to appear in human form. White Snake, appearing thus as beautiful Bai Suzhen (military *dan*), meets the young scholar Xu Xian (*sheng*). The two fall in love and marry, but their happiness is ruined by a Daoist Abbot who objects to the idea of a snake, however cultivated, and a human living together. White Snake overcomes most of the Abbot's military and magical henchmen, but is eventually defeated. The transcription and recorded extract show an early episode where Xu Xian, having visited his parents' graves, is about to encounter White Snake. To a percussion accompaniment, Xu Xian walks dispiritedly onto the stage. The chorus introduce the scene and Xu's mood, then he himself does likewise.

Translation

Chorus: Dark clouds cover the sky and all is dim,
He returns from his ancestral altars and wishes to die;

Xu Xian: Spattered with mud, doused with rain,
Cold rain and warm mud soak my jacket.
My heart is heavy, my future bleak.

Structure

The scene opening transcribed is through-composed, combining passages of song with speech and action. Most song elements consist of couplets – two lines, normally of seven syllables each, possibly enlivened by the insertion of vocables (syllables without grammatical meaning in this context, inserted to spin out the melody further).

Typical of this is the couplet sung by the chorus (of two female singers) at the opening of this scene. This song uses a heptatonic scale (D, E, F, G, A, B, C) with D as fundamental and A as secondary cadential note. (All pitches are a semitone lower on the recording.) The first line (bars 2–5) begins in the high register and ends on the fifth degree of the mode (A). The second line (bars 6–12) is more drawn out through use of vocables. It begins where the first ended, on A, and eventually cadences on the fundamental (D). Xu Xian's words share the same broad structure, but do so more freely, the singer giving two lines (bars 13–21) to the movement towards A and one line (bars 22–26) to the move from A (an octave higher) to the final D. In the text, Xu Xian also spends two lines describing the scene and one introducing his mood; thus, the musical structure follows the structure of the text.

China / Tibet

Tibetan Ritual Music

Cultural background

The region of Tibet is currently part of the People's Republic of China, but important aspects of Tibetan culture remain distinct from those of China, and many Tibetans live in neighbouring countries. One significant difference between Tibet and China is the form of Buddhism practised by many Tibetans, which has more in common with Indian or Central Asian Buddhism than that found in China.

Apart from various forms of religious music, Tibetans have many types of traditional music-making, including folk song, theatrical dance and song styles, entertainment pieces for a mixed ensemble of instruments and voices, and pieces for oboe and drum band. One of the most interesting is the epic song recitation practised by wandering bards.

There are several different schools of Tibetan Buddhism, but the musical customs of each have certain common features. For instance, musical performance is an integral part of daily ceremonies and the less frequent rituals and festivals. Also, this music is performed by specialist priests and monks, not by a lay congregation. The recording used here is an extract from a special ritual dedicated to a female deity known as the Venerable Diamond Yoghini. Apart from processional music, hymns and chanted scriptures, Tibetan Buddhist services such as this one often include passages performed by a group of percussion and wind instruments. Services contain a variety of timbres: loud passages for instrumental ensemble answered by soft chants; periods of solo recitation followed by choral singing; sustained monotones contrasted with fast, wider-ranging melodies; unaccompanied chants alternated with those accompanied by regular patterns on the cymbals and bass drum.

Tibetan Ritual

Instrumentation

The recorded extract is performed by a male soloist and a chorus of male and female voices, all of whom are monks or nuns. Others perform in the instrumental group: *rgya-gling* oboes with seven finger-holes and one thumb-hole; *rkang-gling* trumpet made of human thigh bone or *dung* bass trumpet made of copper or brass; *rol-mo* or *gsil-snyam* cymbals, loud and soft respectively, the leading instrument in this ensemble; *rnga* double-headed frame drum struck with a curved stick; *damaru* hourglass rattle drums, the beaters for which hang from cords on the drum-heads and strike only when the handle of the drum is spun; and *dril-bu* handbells. (The trumpets, used especially at the opening of ceremonies, are not heard on the recorded excerpt.)

Overall, there is a feeling of antiphony between instrumental and vocal sections. Within the former, a heterophonic melody is performed by the *rgya-gling* oboes. This is sometimes accompanied by pedal notes from the trumpets. The percussion instruments have set patterns and styles of performances, including gradually accelerating patterns played on the *rnga* drum.

Mode and structure

In some services a single tonal centre is shared by both instrumental and vocal sections. In this example, the *rgya-gling* perform a four-note melody using the notes F, G, A and B (transcription section 2). The sung chant (section 4) also uses a four-note set but it is quite a different one: G♯, B, C♯ and D♯. Indeed, in the sung passage it is rare to hear all four notes in the same phrase. This narrow contour is typical of Tibetan religious music.

A complete service has an additive structure of instrumental and vocal sections as described above. Within each section, short melodic motifs are typically repeated over and over, sometimes in varied or ornamented form. Section 4 of the transcription illustrates this process, closing with phrases using the arch-shape melodic pattern G♯, B, C♯, B. This pattern is ended in two ways, either falling back to G♯ or remaining on B. Another pattern from this section has a similar contour: B, C♯, D♯, B. Such features as these give the music small-scale stylistic consistency. Larger-scale unity is created through the repetition of chant melodies and instrumental passages throughout a service, although this is not found in every performance.

Transmission

A form of music notation is generally used by the specialist monk responsible for training novices, although it is not referred to during services. Apart from chant texts, the notation contains symbols signifying the style of chanting to be adopted, and prescribed performance techniques. Some chanted passages reiterate meaningless syllables or repeat the name of a particular divinity; others use existing sacred texts.

Diphonic Singing

Cultural background

Mongolian musical culture is not confined to the country of Mongolia itself. Many Mongols live in the People's Republic of China, and culturally-related groups are found from Siberia to Kazakhstan. One such example are the Kalmyk people, who live at the extreme west of the Mongolian-influenced zone: around the southern Ural Mountains and also west of the Caspian Sea not far from Georgia and Armenia. The song studied below is a Kalmyk song of a type shared by Mongolian peoples in general, incorporating a technique variously called diphonic, biphonic and overtone singing.

Vocal music is of principal importance throughout the Mongolian cultural area, although instrumental pieces are performed and instruments sometimes accompany vocal pieces. Traditional Mongolian songs may be divided in several ways. Taking performance style, there are two basic categories: the long and the short song. The former are melismatic and free-rhythmed, the latter syllabic and strictly rhythmic. Taking subject matter, however, there are four main song types: epic songs detailing the life of historical and mythical characters; teaching songs, which may be influenced by Buddhism or, more recently, communism; ritual songs derived from Shamanistic practices; and entertainment songs, a broad category which may include celebratory songs, praise songs and, in some areas, songs performed to enliven manual work. Over the last eighty years, in many of the areas where Mongolian musicians reside, new forms of conservatory-written music have begun to replace the traditional orally-transmitted forms. The recorded piece is a traditional short song of the entertainment type.

Overtone singing

This song demonstrates the celebrated Mongolian technique of singing two pitches simultaneously. As is well known, what we hear as a single musical pitch actually consists of a fundamental note accompanied by a series of higher-pitch 'overtones' or 'partials'. Overtones are softer than the fundamental note, so we do not normally hear them as individual sounds. Instead, they contribute to the timbre of the fundamental, since different instruments or singing techniques favour some overtones more than others. However, in some cases we can hear them clearly – as when a violinist lightly stops a string to play in harmonics, or in Mongolian singing.

The overtones for any note form a regular pattern, although the exact pitches are dictated by the vibrating frequency of the fundamental pitch:

Overtone Series on the Pitch d

Mongolian singers have a number of ways of producing overtones whilst singing. Common to these is the production of a low drone note, often with a rough tone quality. Whilst sustaining this note, the singer then modifies the position of the tongue in the vocal cavity, and perhaps the tension of the vocal chords, to emphasize one or another harmonic overtone of the fundamental drone. Some of these techniques are easy to learn and exciting to experiment with, but it is also possible to damage the vocal chords through over-use.

Short song

The song transcribed consists of eight phrases with a short breath between each. Phrases 1–3 are strongly rhythmic, being a quick chant on two notes a fourth apart (with one exception). One note is given to each syllable. Unfortunately, no translation of the text is available. Phrases 4–8a are sung without text, and consist of free-time melismatic improvisations to different vowel sounds within the overtone register, over a drone note. Notice how the overtone melody in each phrase has an arch structure beginning and ending on D. In phrase 8b the singer returns to the opening rhythmic style but uses the vocal quality of phrases 4–8a, thus appearing to maintain the harmonics as well.

Although the singer slides up a semitone (from D♭ to D), perhaps as a result of tightening the throat in preparation for the diphonic passage, this feature should not be heard as a change of mode. Instead, there is a degree of flexibility in terms of absolute pitch in this style with D (or D♭) being the fundamental note of the overtones and the chanted section. Since the song is performed without instrumental accompaniment, this flexibility creates no problems. Other notes follow the harmonics of the overtone series, omitting those which fall outside a pentatonic scale beginning on D: D, E, F♯, A (also used in the chant) and B.

Music for *Dan Tranh*

Cultural background

Vietnam lies on the boundaries of East and South East Asia. For a long time dominated by China, Vietnam absorbed aspects of Chinese philosophy, literature and music, including instruments and modal systems. During certain periods, Indian and South East Asian cultural influences reached Vietnam, and more recently French and American cultures have had some impact there. Nonetheless, Vietnamese music is not simply a synthesis of foreign elements; there remain distinct regional styles, and amongst the sizeable minority populations quite divergent musical practices.

Vietnamese musical culture reminds us that musical transmission rarely means the complete adoption of a foreign musical style by an indigenous musician, and is related to economic and political factors as much as geographical ones. Even when instruments and tunes are imported, the instruments may be added to pre-existing ensembles and the foreign tunes adapted to local modes and metres. New or local performance techniques may be applied to an imported instrument.

The *dan tranh* illustrates these points, being the Vietnamese form of a zither-type instrument found throughout East Asia. It is played in various types of ensemble – for instance in the group which accompanies Vietnamese theatre, and in *nhac tai tu* chamber music, where *dan tranh*, *dan gao* two-stringed fiddle and *dan kim* two-stringed lute accompany a vocalist. It is also a popular solo instrument.

Performance technique

The wooden body of the *dan tranh* is hollow. One end rests on the kneeling performer's lap, the other on the floor. Traditionally there are sixteen strings, now steel but previously silk or brass. Each is stretched over its own bridge. When the strings are tuned to the notes of a pentatonic scale, a three-octave range is possible. By shifting the bridges, the player re-tunes the instrument to a different mode. The performer's right hand plucks the strings on one side of the bridges; on the other side the left hand presses on the strings to alter or decorate the notes.

Most notes are sounded by plucking with the right thumb or forefinger, although in some regions of Vietnam the middle finger may also be used. The player wears small plectra of curved tortoise-shell, metal or plastic – but occasionally the fingernails are used, giving a different sound.

The main role of the left hand is the alteration of pitch. By pressing a string beyond its bridge, its tension increases and pitch rises, making possible notes not available on the open strings. Also, the performer can move smoothly from one pitch to another by plucking a pressed string and gradually relaxing the left-hand pressure. Thirdly, left-hand pressure fluctuations provide vibrato and other ornamentation. Ornamentational skills are important, with Vietnamese musicians traditionally valued more for their interpretation of a tune than for the number of tunes they know.

Mode and temperament

As in China, Vietnamese music theory describes most music as arising from seven-note scales, of which five notes are essential and the other two typically decorations of other notes rather than independent pitches in themselves. Several different modes are found in Vietnamese traditional music, but the *dieu nam* is one of the most common:

Dieu Nam **with Optional Heptatonic Notes (in black)**

In this mode, the most important notes are the first, fourth and fifth (A, D and E in the example above); most phrases begin and end with one of these notes. Theoretically, this mode can begin on any of the twelve semitones, not just A, but some absolute tunings are more commonly used than others. Some Far Eastern musicians have been aware of equal temperament (the sub-division of the octave into twelve identically-sized semitones) for as long as Western musicians, but until the impact of Western music education and popular music broadcasts, they preferred semitone intervals of slightly different sizes. In traditional *dieu nam* music, the fourth note seems a little sharp to Western ears, and the third and sixth vary quite widely from one school of performance to another.

Contrasting patterns of ornamentation are used in each mode. This, with the particular choice of primary notes, differing cadential emphasis and idiosyncratic modal temperaments make music in one mode sound very different from that in another.

 Track 9

Khong Minh toa lau

The title of this short composition for solo *dan tranh* can be translated 'Khong Minh Sits on the Balcony'. It presents the same theme three times, to demonstrate some of the instrument's performing techniques and sonorities. There is also an introductory passage which establishes the mode of the piece. The first version of the theme (section 2, bars 7–18) is presented in octaves, often syncopated, and elaborated with glissando strums across several strings. The second version (section 3, bars 19–30) has fewer glissando runs but more use of the left-hand decorative pressing technique. A third and final version (not transcribed) omits octave doubling and features harmonics. There are also melodic and rhythmic alterations from one variation to the next.

Work Song

Cultural background

In many countries, people recognize different categories of folk songs. In Vietnam, some of the main types are work songs, love songs, lullabies, poetic recitation, ceremonial songs, cult songs, festival songs, pedlars' songs and children's songs, though these categories may not be mutually exclusive. Many different peoples inhabit Vietnam, and there is considerable regional difference in terms of culture and language, so folk-singing style within these categories can differ quite widely from place to place. In this case, a central Vietnamese work song has been chosen for study.

Vietnamese work songs

There are several contrasting kinds of work song in Vietnam. Traditionally, they accompany activities such as dragging wood, rowing boats and planting rice. Most work songs are called *ho*, which comes from the word meaning 'to raise the voice'. Some *ho* are designed to match the rhythm and patterns of manual labour – useful when multiple workers need to synchronize their movements. Others are sung during rest periods and some at singing contests held at traditional festivals during the year.

Work songs often involve repetition of text and melodic patterns. Since parts of them are sung by several people together, melodic range is typically fairly narrow, and the melody restricted to a few notes. These songs are also characterized by the use of vocables: nonsense syllables and phrases, often featuring aspirated consonants such as *ho* to ensure that all those working take the strain together. Lyrics are normally in pairs of lines: solo (call) and group (response).

Such songs were often improvised during performance, the leader creating new phrases to a well-known traditional melody and the chorus repeating a few simple words or nonsense syllables. In some songs, the leader's text concentrates on directing the work at hand. However, it is equally possible for a lead singer to entertain his fellows with a story, poem, scenic description or love song. No instrumental accompaniment is used.

Mode

Different modes are employed in folk singing in various parts of Vietnam. Central Vietnamese folk singers regularly use a form of the *dieu nam* (see Vietnam: Music for *Dan Tranh*). This consists of these relative pitches: do, re (a little flat), fa (quite variable in pitch and sung with vibrato), sol and la (a little flat). In the accompanying transcription, the pitch 'do' is equivalent to the note F.

Track 10

Ho hui

This style of work song is typical of central Vietnam. *Ho hui*, 'Soil-Flattening Call', was a song form originated by masons, its fast and regular rhythm matching the beating of the soil by the team of workers. This rhythm leads to a regular metrical organization, with a single exception towards the middle of the song.

The overall structure of the song is ternary, as shown below:

Bars	Material	Comments
1–4	I	Introduction: two couplets of solo call and group response; text mostly vocables
5–14	A	Verse 1: two solo lines, interrupted and answered by group phrases. Rounded off by a couplet of vocables from **I**
14–23	B	Episode: higher-register, contrasting section of three pairs of call and response using vocables, including 'ho hui'. Rounded off by the couplet that ended **I** and **A**
24–33	A'	Verse 2: as **A**.

In a longer performance, this structure could be extended through repetition of further pairs of sections **B** and **A**. Repetition of section **B** allows the leader time to think up new words for the next verse. The same group phrase 'La huc la khoan' is used after every solo line in the introduction and verses, and the same solo vocable phrase 'A ly khoan ho khoan' completes each song section. Repetition of this sort makes it easier for the chorus to sing whilst working. On the other hand, the lead singer varies the melody of every phrase of text, following the contour of the words.

Translation

I	I ask you, friend,
A	Do you know? Up until February, Women plant the rice, Men plough the fields.
A'	Above the field is shallow, Below the field is deep. The husband ploughs and the wife plants, The son digs.

(All vocables omitted)

Music for *Khaēn*

Cultural background

The *khaēn* is a free-reed mouth organ, one of the most characteristic instruments of traditional Laotian culture. It is also popular in north-eastern Thailand, where many Laotian people live, and related instruments occur across South East and East Asia. The *khaēn* has a range of different functions and can be heard in a wide variety of contexts. In past times, it was important as a therapeutic aid for labourers in the fields, and was also played by young men travelling in search of wives. As a result of urbanization and industrialization, the solo *khaēn* is mainly heard today as entertainment at private celebrations and public festivals. It also accompanies traditional Laotian singing, which includes theatrical music, non-theatrical styles and the *mawlum pee fah* ceremony to appease spirits believed to be causing illness.

The *khaēn*

The origin of the instrument is uncertain; few accounts of Laotian music predate the nineteenth century, and very few historical or archaeological specimens of these bamboo instruments are available. A *khaēn* is constructed from two parallel rows of bamboo pipes which pass through a barrel-shaped, wooden wind-chest and are sealed in place by a black, sticky caulking substance. The number of pipes varies widely: a *khaēn hok* (literally 'six *khaēn*'), has six pipes in two parallel rows of three, whilst a *khaēn jet* ('seven') has two parallel rows of seven pipes, or fourteen in all. The standard instrument today, the *khaēn baet* ('eight'), has sixteen pipes in two parallel rows of eight. Pipe-length is commonly around one metre, but contrasts according to the function of the instrument and the player's personal preference.

Each pipe has a free-reed, perhaps of copper or silver, which vibrates at a fixed frequency. Air passes through all the pipes, but a small finger-hole above the wind-chest in each pipe interrupts the column of air, preventing each reed from vibrating until the specific finger-hole is covered. Two further holes are cut into each pipe, one at the top and one below the wind-chest. These are 'pitch-holes' and influence the tuning of the instrument. In performance, the *khaēn* is played by inhaling and exhaling through the mouthpiece on the wind-chest, which is cupped by the palms.

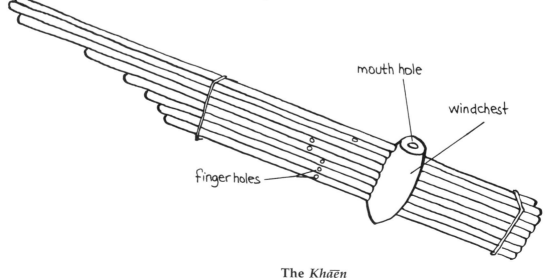

The *Khaēn*

The music of the
khaēn

The music of the *khaēn* is passed on through listening to and observing other players in an entirely oral tradition. No form of musical notation exists – *khaēn* music is composed in performance by improvisation. The sound details of each performance of a so-called 'piece' will differ, but the music follows a system with internal logic and structure, which the player must understand before performing in public. There is no standardization in the form or length of a *khaēn* improvisation, such factors being left to the discretion of the player, who will usually adapt an improvisation according to taste and performance context. Some performances are very short, lasting only a minute or two, but longer improvisations can take the form of a suite with several sections.

Tuning and mode

There is no standard absolute tuning for the *khaēn*, although the notes usually form a similar pattern of intervals. On the *khaēn baet* the notes available are approximately equivalent to those of the Western natural minor scale, with seven different pitches to each octave. However, most music relies on one or another pentatonic mode:

Typical Pentatonic Modes in Music for *Khaēn*

Apart from using different sets of notes and cadencing to different fundamental pitches, each mode differs in the range of notes used, the use of note-clusters (the addition of other notes to a single melodic line) and the employment of characteristic melodic phrases and cadential figures. The drone notes are the fundamental (which is not necessarily the lowest note) and the note a fifth above or a fourth below.

 *Track 11*

Nam phat khay

This improvisation, 'In the Current of the Mekong', uses the mode B, D, E, F♯ and A over the whole two-octave range of notes available on the *khaēn baet*. B (the fundamental) and F♯ are sounded throughout as drone notes. The three lowest notes (B, D and E) are regularly doubled an octave higher. Apart from these octave-doublings and the frequent addition of the note A to the octave D pair, note-clusters are rare in this mode.

Nam phat khay has been transcribed in duple metre. This is because the performance technique of regular inhaling and exhaling typically produces a feeling of rhythmic couplets. Material can also be 'borrowed' from other improvisations in the same mode, for instance the phrase which occurs in bars 9, 17 and elsewhere. Structure is additive, with short patterns and melodies being assembled one by one into a longer piece. These features make it a typical example of improvisatory *khaēn* music. The transcription shows the opening of a four-minute piece.

Indonesia

Javanese Dance-Opera

Cultural background

Java is one of the most remarkable cultural centres of South East Asia. One of the principal islands constituting Indonesia, it was Hindu until the fifteenth century, when Islam became predominant. Contemporary Javanese culture combines indigenous features with elements of both these religious traditions, the more general influences of Arabic, Indian and South East Asian culture, and certain aspects of East Asian and European artistic styles.

Amongst Java's many musical forms, that for ensembles called *gamelan* is now known world-wide. In Europe, concert-style *gamelan* performances are usual, but within Indonesia the music is more typically the accompaniment to nocturnal shadow-puppetry, dance or theatre. The example transcribed is a setting of the traditional Ramayana myth, but is unusual in that it presents music from a rare style of dance-opera invented at the end of the nineteenth century and only recently revived.

Although sometimes likened to an orchestra, the *gamelan* is not an assemblage of instruments which may also be played solo. Instead, the Javanese term *gamelan*, derived from 'to hammer', usually refers to a set of bronze gongs, drums and xylophones plus a few other instruments such as the spike fiddle, all of which are generally joined by singers in performance. Several instruments in this set have extensive histories, and the set as a whole is considered a special, symbolic item. Good performers can play most of the instruments in the *gamelan* set, adding stylish decorations in performance to complete a memorized musical outline.

Instrumentation

The instruments used in a large contemporary Javanese *gamelan* are of several different types. There are two basic categories of metal instruments: sets of tuned bars, and individual or multiple knobbed gongs. The former include the *saron*, *gender* and *slentem*. The *saron* usually have seven smooth bars set into a hollow wooden frame which acts as a resonator. There are three sizes, tuned an octave apart. The *gender* and *slentem* have ribbed rather than smooth bars, and are suspended by cords above a wooden frame supporting a row of carefully-tuned resonating tubes. There are two types of *gender*, again an octave apart, while the *slentem* sounds an octave lower again. The main melody of a *gamelan* piece is performed on *saron* and *slentem*, usually somewhat ornamented on the highest *saron*. The *gender*, on the other hand, play accompanying patterns.

Gong-type instruments include large, stand-suspended instruments and smaller gongs resting in wooden frames. Generally, the former are struck regularly to punctuate the music and mark progression through each phrase. Principal amongst these is the low-pitched *gong ageng* 'large gong', which is sounded once to end each section. Frame-supported gongs include further periodically-played accompaniment gongs, and also two *bonang*, two-octave gong-sets tuned an octave apart which perform interlocking patterns around and above the main melody.

Passing over less significant metal instruments, several wooden ones are also important, for instance the xylophone *gambang*. Played mostly in parallel octaves, this provides a faster, decorated form of the melody over a wide range. The melody is also played, very freely, by the two-stringed spike fiddle *rebab* and the end-blown flute *suling*. The *rebab*, considered a leading instrument, normally maintains a sustained sound, while the *suling* typically plays short, intermittent phrases. A principal role is also accorded to the *kendang*, three or four wooden, double-headed barrel drums, struck with the hands. Standardized *kendang* patterns accompany many simple pieces and songs. In theatre and dance, more complex techniques are employed. Whatever the genre, drum signals control the start and finish of each piece and indicate tempo, dynamics and repeats.

Finally, several voice-types are added to these instrumental sonorities. Typical vocal timbres are a solo female voice, ornamenting the main melody; a chorus of several male singers, who perform a unison, simpler version of the melody; and the *dalang* narrator, who speaks and sings in shadow-puppet plays.

Tuning and mode

Two tuning systems are found in *gamelan* ensembles: *slendro*, in which the octave is divided into five roughly equal parts, and *pelog*, where seven notes are unevenly spaced throughout the octave (though not all are used in each *pelog* piece). In contemporary notation the seven *pelog* notes are written as 1, 2, 3, 4, 5, 6 and 7, while the pentatonic *slendro* pitches are labelled 1, 2, 3, 5 and 6. Each tuning system has several different modes, which differ in both emphasis and avoidance of specific pitches. Emphasis results from placing important pitches at phrase ends and through repetition, for example. The transcribed excerpt uses a mode which emphasises note 5 and avoids note 3.

 *Track 12*

Langen Mandra Wanara

The transcribed excerpt from the dance-opera *Langen Mandra Wanara*, an episode from the Ramayana, shows a passage of narration and the *rebab*-led start of a pre-existent *gamelan* tune, 'Gending ladrang Sri Hascarya'. *Gending* in this context means 'composition', while *ladrang* signifies a piece structured in 32-beat sections. *Sri Hascarya*, 'The Light of Joy', is the title of the specific piece itself. The narration has been transcribed in staff notation and the beginning of the *gamelan* piece in contemporary Javanese cipher notation.

In metred Javanese *gamelan* music like this, metrical emphasis is placed on the fourth beat of each unit. The note of the main melody which falls on the fourth beat is doubled on the deeper gongs, and is treated as a melodic target by musicians playing the most ornamented parts. Other gong-strokes are reserved for every second or every fourth unit, or even further apart. Above these are instruments sounded once or twice within each four-beat unit; and then those which typically play a single note of the main melody to each beat. Above these again are instruments and voices performing simple variations or repetitions of melodic notes; then those which produce decorative or accompanying patterns; and also the rhythmic support of the *kendang* drum. At the very top of the texture are very fast versions of the theme, ornamented with complex interlocking patterns.

Summary-translation of the text

Narrator (declaiming):
For some time, Baron Lesmana and King Sugriwa, followed by the ape army, have journeyed to Maliawan. When they appear in the distance the musicians play 'Gending ladrang Sri Hascarya' to welcome them.
(The text of the gending is not translated)

Balinese Music for *Gamelan Gong Gede*

Cultural background

Bali lies east of Java in the Indonesian islands. Since the fourteenth century, important cultural influences have come from Java, with developments in Javanese music broadly paralleled in Bali. Many Hindu Javanese nobles, anxious to avoid the Islamification of Java, moved to Bali, taking their court musicians, dancers and actors. The ensemble of bronze instruments known as *gamelan* developed over this same period. By the beginning of the nineteenth century, more than a dozen different kinds of *gamelan* orchestra were found in Bali, and the number and size of instruments, their tuning and scales, their repertories and functions continues to vary to the present day. The type recorded here is a *gamelan gong gede*, a large set of instruments now unusual in Bali. More typical might have been an example of the exuberant and virtuoso *gong kebyar* style. Performers are typically members of amateur music clubs which meet for pleasure and because music has an important function in Balinese society. Some of these musicians use a form of cipher notation (see Indonesia: Javanese Dance-Opera) but most learn by rote, rehearsals perhaps taking the form of experienced musicians playing through a composition over and over again as the rest gradually pick it up.

Religion is an integral part of community life in traditional Balinese villages, and musical performance an essential part of religious observances. Most villages have several temples where music and dance are regularly performed. Two types of music are found in these ceremonies: music which introduces, accompanies or connects different parts of a ritual, and music played specifically for the pleasure of the gods (as well as a Balinese audience). Both fast and slow pieces are found. Transitional compositions, such as the excerpt transcribed, tend to be faster and briefer in structure than those designed primarily for entertainment and may also be played by the *gong kebyar* ensemble to accompany dance and theatre.

Instrumentation

The Balinese *gamelan gong gede*, or 'great *gamelan*', is a large set of bronze metallophones, primarily of the xylophone type or knobbed and bulbed gongs. To these are added a *suling* end-blown flute, cymbals, and a pair of *kendang* drums. A principal melodic instrument is the *trompong*, a line of ten bulbed gongs struck with mallets. A second *trompong* doubles the melody of the first an octave higher. Also important are the *reyong*, a set of six or twelve gongs played in interlocking melodic patterns by multiple performers, and a xylophone-type instrument with eleven tuned bars, the *kantilan*.

Melody and structure

The basis of a Balinese *gamelan* composition is a so-called 'nuclear melody'. This is punctuated by one or more gongs, and animated by drumming. The term 'nuclear melody' refers to a basic melodic outline; this contains the musical material from which a complete piece is fleshed out during performance. Balinese musical form is based on elements called *tabuh*, the chief characteristics of which are their melodic shape, pattern of large gong beats, and overall number of beats. Complete compositions have solo introductions, and range from the performance of a single *tabuh* to works of great breadth with a number of movements.

 *Track 13*

Tabuh Pisan

This particular composition, *Tabuh Pisan*, is introduced by a passage on the *kendang* drum. This is followed by the first *tabuh*, which features an acceleration to double speed before slowing down again. A longer, melodically-contrasting *tabuh* follows. Finally, there is a return to the opening *tabuh*, giving the piece an overall ternary form. The transcription shows the whole of the first *tabuh* and part of the second. Within each *tabuh*, certain phrases may be repeated, as in the first section:

Bars	Phrase	Comments
1–4	a	opening phrase: establishes mode and set of notes used, and begins acceleration
5–8	a'	varied repeat
9–12	b	contrasting phrase opening up the upper register. note how bars 11–12 are a syncopated version of 9–10
13–16	c	new contrasting phrase using the upper register
17–20	d	phrase using the lower register – the first phrase to start on a note other than D
21–24	e	new phrase, beginning on D
25–28	d'	varied repeat of 17–20. Start of deceleration
29–32	e'	varied repeat of 21–24
33–37	d"	varied repeat of 17–20, extended by one bar to cadence onto D

Five pitches are used in this composition, approximately equivalent to D, E, F, A and B (but a semitone lower on the recording), with D as the fundamental note. Although this can be described as a pentatonic scale, to the music theorist this is a five-note subset of the heptatonic *pelog* tuning system (see Indonesia: Javanese Dance-Opera). This set of five notes differs from the Balinese *slendro* pentatonic tuning system in that the gaps between adjacent pitches in the former vary from a semitone (E–F) to a major third (F–A) while in the latter each interval is approximately the same.

Philippines

Palawan Love Song

Cultural background

The music of the Philippines contains immense variety and interest. In some remote areas there are traditions and instruments similar to those of Oceania. In regions closer to Indonesia there are many aspects of 'gong-culture'. Elsewhere the colonial Spanish influence remains marked, and in many towns and cities various forms of American popular music are maintained. There are also Philippine composers working in Western classical idioms and South East Asian pop styles, amongst others. This is not to say that Philippine music is just an amalgam of foreign influences – at least not any more than in most other parts of the world. Once external forms, instruments and styles are adopted and adapted for local use, they come to belong to the people who use them.

We examine here the musical traditions of a small tribe who inhabit a forested highland region on the western island of Palawan. The musical culture of these people is distinct from those of their neighbours, but also shares several elements with them. For instance, the highlanders have a small type of gong and drum ensemble similar to some in other parts of South East Asia, which perform music of highly-organized rhythmic complexity but little melodic content. Apart from these, the vocal and instrumental music of the Palawan highlands employs such instruments as the *suling* vertical flute (see Indonesia: Javanese Dance-Opera), the *aruding* jaw's harp (found across Oceania), the *kusyapiq* two-stringed lute (forms of which occur in many parts of South East Asia) and the *pagang* bamboo tube zither (also widely distributed). Instruments are played for pleasure, and are used to accompany love songs, historical and mythical tales (which may last several nights) and ceremonials. Much entertainment singing is connected with the lore of the forest and its wildlife.

Instrumentation

The transcribed excerpt features two of these instruments, the *kusyapiq* and *pagang*, as the accompaniment to alternating male and female solo voices. The male singer performs the *kusyapiq* and the woman the *pagang*.

The *kusyapiq* lute has a boat-like soundbox and a long neck. As with many Western stringed instruments, it is described anthropomorphically, having an 'ear', 'head', 'neck' and 'chest', amongst other parts which mark it as being a male instrument. This symbolism is sometimes taken further, holes on the rear of the box being carved into a man's silhouette. There are two strings, one of which is plucked as a rhythmic drone. The other, used to play melodies, has half a dozen frets, which can be adjusted in position to allow performance in two differently-spaced pentatonic scales. The first, used for instrumental pieces, divides the octave into five broadly equivalent steps. The other, used in *kulilal* love songs, contains two steps of a semitone, one of a tone and two major thirds.

The *pagang* is constructed from a wide tube of bamboo. Eight or nine strings are stretched the length of the tube, which rests upright on the player's lap during performance. The strings are plucked with the fingers and thumbs of both hands, the hollow tube acting as a resonator.

Kulilal songs

Kulilal songs are an ensemble art form, typically requiring the participation of at least one male *kusyapiq* player and one female *pagang* zither performer. Singing in turn, and possibly incorporating couplets sung by listeners seated nearby, the performers weave a web of poetic allusions and emotional appeals toward those they love. Each of the singers will probably be directing their words to a different person, and since the Palawan couch their terms of endearment in highly-veiled phrases, and because song-style transforms the language used, it may be impossible for any one listener to completely understand the text of a specific *kulilal* song. Archaic words and words borrowed from neighbouring tribes are used, pronunciations are adjusted and grammatical elements omitted.

① Track 14

Kulilal at puguq

The excerpt transcribed from the 'Love Song of the Quail' illustrates some of the features of this musical style. The text (translated below) appears to show two singers hinting at locations special to themselves and their respective beloveds. Each line of text has six syllables, with the ends of lines being open to extension with extra vocables.

The music relies on a four-bar instrumental passage which is repeated over and over. Vocal parts are then fitted in with the instrumental melody as appropriate. The music may be described as using 8/8 metre, rather like 4/4 time but with more flexible patterns of emphasis, resulting in what may seem like syncopation to the Western listener. Only four pitches are used: D (the bass drone note) and its neighbour C♯, and A and its neighbour G♯. Technically the pitch E is possible in this tuning as well, but it does not appear in this song.

Translation

Three couplets are transcribed, from a complete song of seven couplets:

Male: Two trunks of the palm tree,
          Two trunks of the palm tree, [vocables].

          O yes I know it,
          O yes I know it,

Female: [vocables: O yes].

          A weir of stones,
          A weir of stones,   [vocables].

Music for *Aruding*

Cultural background

The Palawan of the Philippines (see Philippines: Palawan Love Song), in common with many traditionally non-literate peoples, preserve much of their lore in song or musical form. In the case of the Palawan, the many natural sounds of the forest surrounding their fields and homes provide a rich resource of musical stimuli. Music psychologists have commented that one reason why humans have music is that it is easier to memorize and recollect information when it is attached to melody or rhythmic patterns. A second explanation for human music-making is that for many peoples, music is a way of relating human society to the broader natural and supernatural worlds. Musical performance does not simply retrieve stored information, it transforms it in special and significant ways. For example, among the peoples of Oceania, with whom the Palawan have certain affinities, musical compositions imitating the sounds of birds, insects or animals may be seen as a way of communicating with animal spirits, gods, mythical ancestors or the recently dead. The piece transcribed combines several of these themes, being a composition reminding listeners of the mythical origins of a particular species of bird and its ominous call.

The *aruding*

The example of Palawan instrumental music transcribed is performed on the bamboo *aruding* jaw's harp. The *aruding* consists of a length of bamboo with a section cut to resemble a thin tongue. The bamboo tongue is plucked with a finger while the instrument is gripped in the mouth. A single fundamental pitch is produced, but this pitch is accompanied by a series of overtones or harmonics (see Mongolia: Diphonic Singing). By control of the vocal cavity and tongue position, the musician can cause one or other of these harmonics to ring out particularly prominently. The performer can also quickly move from one harmonic to its neighbour on a single pluck. As a result, the listener hears both the fundamental as a kind of rhythmically-reiterated drone bass and a more melodic succession of different harmonics.

Track 15

Lumalibang

The 'Red-Headed Whistler' is a forest bird the Palawan credit with human origins. To Palawan listeners its cry is of ill omen, announcing the death of a distant man. Birds appear to occupy a prominent place in Palawan cosmology and music-making, the songs of many different types being imitated or represented in music and their cries being held to have various meanings. Despite all this symbolism, however, this music is also played for entertainment and personal contemplation.

In musical terms, *Lumalibang* consist of three elements or note-groups:

Three Musical Elements in *Lumalibang*

These elements are combined throughout the short composition as follows:

a		b	c
a			c
a	a	b	c

The opening consists of the pattern **a b c; a c** (repeated once) but thereafter the music settles down to repeat the longer pattern **a a b c; a c; a b c**. All elements are begun by a pluck on the *aruding* which yields the sounds of a fundamental A and its harmonic C♯. In the case of elements **a** and **b**, the player alters the vocal cavity to create a legato movement to the next upper harmonic, E. In element **c**, melodic direction is reversed, with legato movement approaching the neighbouring lower harmonic, A. Element **b** consists of just the single pluck and the harmonics C♯ and E, but in elements **a** and **c** a second pluck reiterates the fundamental and the second harmonic pitch.

Since all harmonics are given approximately equal duration, the alternation of elements **a** and **c** (with three harmonics) with element **b** (two harmonics), added to the fast speed of performance, creates a complex metrical effect. This is underlined by the rhythm of the plucked notes: long/short in elements **a** and **c** but simply long in element **b**. In this, the music is similar to other Palawan forms which require few melodic resources but develop considerable rhythmic subtlety. The whole of the piece is given on the transcription and accompanying recording.

Rihe Panpipe Ensemble

Cultural background
The Solomon Islands, part of a series of islands collectively referred to as Melanesia, lie in the Pacific Ocean to the east of New Guinea and north-east of Australia. One of the principal islands in the Solomon group is Guadalcanal, where the transcribed example of panpipe ensemble music was recorded. Perhaps the most striking feature of musical culture on Guadalcanal is the great importance of instrumental music as compared to vocal music. In many other cultures, instruments are used primarily to accompany the voice, or aspire to imitate the voice. However, in this region, voices are sometimes used in ways which imitate the effect of local instrumental ensembles (see Solomon Islands: *Rope* Female Chorus).

Rihe Mumu
Panpipe music in Guadalcanal is held to be a remnant of the culture of the Mumu people, earlier inhabitants of the island. It is performed by men, who add the sound of ten high-pitched *pusu* and *kenge* bamboo whistles with one or two tubes each, and two end-blown *mbangaru* bamboo sound-tubes to a basic quartet of four *rihe* panpipes. A *rihe* consists of two rows of bamboo pipes, with typically fifteen to seventeen pipes in each row. The front row of pipes are blocked at the lower end while the second row are open-ended. Although of similar length, the open-ended pipes sound an octave higher than the closed ones. The pitches available on a row of closed pipes on a typical *rihe* are:

Approximate Closed-Pipe Pitches on a *Rihe*
Arrows show pitches which are sharper or flatter than equal-tempered semitones

The texture which results from this ensemble is complex in several ways. Firstly, the four panpipes are not tuned exactly the same, so a 'thick' sound results when they perform the same note. Secondly, each performer has a different rhythmic and melodic role. Two of the panpipes perform the melody in the lower register, one lagging slightly behind the other. The other two play an octave higher, again in interlocking fashion, and may play variations or a countermelody. Meanwhile, the sound-tube players produce a drone, overlapping their breathing to create a continuous sound, and the whistles add to the texture, yet again in alternation, with shorter, staccato sounds.

 *Track 16*

Kikira

'The Parrot' is a good example of a novel piece for *rihe mumu* ensemble. As in many Solomon Islands compositions, the idea is to imitate a natural sound, in this case the cry of the parrot. To that end, the composer has made some modifications to the usual performance texture. He can do this because although the Solomon Islanders do not use musical notation they do employ a special musical terminology, with specific words for each part and its role in the texture. In this piece, two panpipes interweave a high-register melody above a drone played by the other panpipes and the bamboo sound-tubes. Instead of adding an accompaniment to this, the whistle players portray the intermittent call of the parrot with shrill, piercing tones.

Although the composer was creative with texture, his use of melody is more typical. The melody of *Kikira* consists of short patterns freely used over and over again. Some of these patterns, which last three beats in this piece, are also found in other pieces played by the same musicians. The whole piece consists of three stanzas. The first begins with the parts entering gradually, led by the melody panpipes who begin in the upper register. At the end of the stanza the two higher panpipes descend to double the drone note an octave higher. This stanza is then repeated twice more in varied form, with a codetta figure – also found in other ensemble pieces – rounding off the composition.

Rope Female Chorus

Cultural background

The important position of instrumental music in the Solomon Islands has already been discussed (see Solomon Islands: *Rihe* Panpipe Ensemble). It was noted that vocal music often imitates the sound and texture of instrumental pieces. In fact there may be no song text, so that the listener concentrates on the sound of the voices, not the meaning of the words. The singers remain facially impassive, and there is little use of vibrato or dynamic contrast. Vocal music from this area shares the usual instrumental texture of drone and two melodic parts. A final resemblance between instrumental and vocal music is that both are said by the Solomon Islanders to imitate natural and man-made sounds.

The *rope*

Depending on the region of Guadalcanal, a *rope* is either a circular dance performed at public festivities, or a women's chorus performed either seated at such festivities or less formally to enliven horticultural work. In this case, it is the latter which has been recorded, a song for female singers without either instrumental accompaniment or dance movement. The women sit on the ground to perform. Two of them sing solo, and the remainder (another ten) produce a lower-pitched drone note, staggering their breathing to produce a continuous sound. Several songs are sung in sequence, and the soloists may alter from one to another. Special names are given to each part in this texture.

The solo singers employ two voice qualities in *rope* songs, chest voice and head voice. The tone quality of the latter is quite distinct from the former, though this cannot easily be shown in staff notation. In the example transcribed, notes up to b' are sung with the chest voice whilst high c" and d" use the head voice.

Track 17

Ratsi Rope

The recorded example, literally 'Begin the *Rope*', comes from the start of a sequence of *rope* song performances. It is less complex than some of the other songs in the sequence, which imitate sounds such as bird-song and the herding of pigs. The whole of this song is found on the accompanying recording. It uses the notes of a hexatonic scale (approximately equivalent to): G, A, B, C, E and F♯. G is sustained by the drone-part singers, and is also reached by the two solo singers at the very end of the song.

The two solo parts are fairly independent in rhythmic and melodic character, although both consist at the most fundamental level of a single, four-beat pattern which is repeated over and over in varied form throughout the song. For the first singer, this pattern revolves around the pitch E, whilst the second centres on G. Part of the affect of the song on the Western listener arises from the first soloist's use of the interval between C and F♯, an interval habitually avoided in traditional Western melody-writing. Also fundamental to the style of this music is the singing of several neighbouring pitches at once, for example on the final beat of the introduction where we hear E, F♯ and G simultaneously. Some commentators suggest that the loud performance, without vibrato, of such dissonant note-clusters sets up a very physical 'buzz' or tension in the air. This is periodically resolved as the singers move on to more consonant combinations of pitches, and finally by their closing sustained unison or octave drone. Thus, even though the music is not harmonic in the traditional Western sense, it may rely upon the same fundamental interplay between tension and relaxation.

The voices enter in turn, the first soloist beginning, the second following two beats later and the chorus gradually joining in with the low-pitched drone. The two lead singers then perform fourteen variants of their basic vocal patterns. Finally, the song is concluded by all voices holding the drone note for four beats and then sliding downwards in pitch. Because each vocal pattern lasts four beats, it is convenient to describe the song as having a simple quadruple metre. Nonetheless, the rhythmic subdivision of individual beats within this metre is flexible, with many pairs of notes having a triplet-like lilt.

Arnhem Land Aboriginal Music

Cultural background

Traditional Australian Aboriginal music is intrinsically linked to Aboriginal views of cosmology, religion, ceremony and the general education of society. Australian Aborigines believe that creativity is rooted in the Dreamtime, a mythological period within which the known world was formed. As a result, the creation of songs is ascribed to ancestral beings from the Dreamtime rather than to the people of the present day. These songs are said to be the creation of spirit-familiars, who communicate with their chosen human vessels in dreams.

Unlike in other hunter-gatherer societies, where the most highly-respected person is typically a hunter or food-gatherer, in traditional Aboriginal clans leadership is given to the Songman, or Master of Music. The Songman is responsible for songs containing mythology, folklore, legend and gossip, and the teaching songs that are passed down through generations. The Songman is credited with psychic power, since it is he who is said to learn new songs in dreams and through visitations from spirits.

Arnhem Land is the area to the North of the Northern Territories in Australia. The music of this region falls into three categories: sacred, which includes totemic and heroic cult music; secular; and secret. The song transcribed and recorded illustrates the secular category, which may be performed at any time in camp. Subject matter tends to be commentary on past or present incidents, ballads, natural phenomena and species, and (increasingly) introduced articles such as axes, tobacco, boats and cards. Sung commentary on events or individuals can take a metaphorical form, because Aboriginal society does not encourage the making of direct personal comments. Instead, songs about animals can be used as a veiled means of commenting upon the personality or experiences of a particular individual.

Aboriginal music

Traditional Aboriginal music is primarily vocal, with songs for rain-making, rain-stopping, love-magic and secret incantations. These songs are characterized by non-verbal sounds and syllabic chanting. Non-verbal sounds include grunting, high-pitched falsetto, growling and wailing. Vocal qualities range from low huskiness to high, dynamically-contrasting falsetto. Some songs are for solo voice, others are performed in a heterophonic style, and still more may be sung by different groups simultaneously.

Vocal music can be accompanied by rhythm sticks, drum, and in some areas by striking together pairs of boomerangs. Further percussion instruments are fashioned from bark, seed-pods and fish-skin. The body is also used to provide percussive sounds, such as hand-clapping, or slapping the thighs or buttocks.

An important instrument is the didjeridu, used both for accompaniment and for solo performance. Usually about four or five feet long, and tipped with a mouthpiece of wax or hardened gum, the didjeridu is made from either a hollowed-out branch or a length of bamboo. Performance may require the use of circular breathing (using cheek pressure to exhale from the mouth while quickly inhaling through the nose). The instrument provides a droning sound elaborated by intricate cross-rhythms.

 *Track 18*

Birruck

The birruck is a rock wallaby found in the caves and rocky slopes of Arnhem Land. Ostensibly, *Birruck* tells of a wallaby finding a wild plum tree laden with fruit, but it is possible that this song was originally intended to comment on some person or event known to the singer. The Songman sings four verses accompanied by the didjeridu and rhythm sticks, with short instrumental preludes before each verse. The text of each verse, like many Aboriginal songs, combines phrases of padding syllables with phrases of actual, meaningful text. The didjeridu and rhythm sticks are played continuously. The rhythm sticks provide a steady pulse throughout the piece, supported by a variable drone from the didjeridu. Although there is a steady pulse, there is no sense of a metre in the Western sense, i.e. a patterned succession of strong and weak beats. Nonetheless, many of the repeated vocal rhythms can be conveniently grouped into the equivalent of simple duple time.

In melodic terms, *Birruck* demonstrates a tendency of Arnhem Land songs: to begin on a high note and descend gradually to a lower pitch. This melodic descent is decorated with falling glides and occasional ornamentation. In this case, a hexatonic (six-note) scale of A, C, D, E, F♯ and G is used (approximately a semitone lower on the recording). Each verse consists of a gradual fall from G down to A. The verse can be divided into three parts: reiteration of the pitch G (bars 17–21), descent to and repetition of E (22–28) and the fall to and repetition of A (29–37).

India

Music for *Vīnā*

Cultural background

Indian art music is amongst the best known traditional musical styles world-wide, and has been extensively documented, both by Indian scholars and by foreign musicians. Skilled practitioners now reside in many countries, top soloists tour internationally and recordings are readily available. In these respects, the Indian art music tradition quite closely resembles that of the West. The parallel can be taken a little further. In each case, these are elite traditions with historical roots in religious ceremony and court entertainment. They are both primarily urban styles, performed principally at formal concerts where the roles of performer and listener are clearly demarcated. Both require of would-be professional musicians a long period of specialist study and apprenticeship, and are most deeply appreciated by experienced audiences. Both are accompanied by considerable amounts of written and spoken musical theory and terminology. Supporters of each tradition see their music as being substantially different from – and more valuable than – other musical styles occurring within the same area, such as village bands or popular music. Of course, there are important differences in the sounds and practices of Indian and Western art musics. However, the point is that parallels between these two traditions are not accidental or incidental: they arise from their similar social and historical contexts.

Indian art music

Art music in India is divided into two main types, that of the North and that of the South. Within these two broad categories there is a great deal of local and regional variation. Nonetheless, a few general points can be made. First of all, there are certain parallels in the combinations of instrument-types typically found in both North and South Indian art music. Secondly, much of this music relies upon the combination in performance of memorized compositions and extemporized improvisations. Third, many of these improvisations use modal bases or *rāgas* which provide the player with a set of pitches, certain characteristic ways of proceeding through the set, and an emotional mood to keep in mind. Typically, the accompaniment to such music will include a sustained drone note, the fundamental of the mode in question. Finally, musicians use a wide range of metrical structures as well as passages of 'free-time' performance.

The *vīnā*

The recorded music is an example of performance on the *vīnā*, a South Indian form of lute with a rounded body and long, fretted neck. A second resonator, perhaps a gourd, is attached to the upper part of the neck, beneath the tuning pegs. The *vīnā* is held diagonally across the body of the cross-legged player, its body resting beside the right knee and second resonator supported by the left knee. The fingers of the right hand are used to strike the strings, while the left hand takes care of stopping the strings, possibly ornamenting sustained notes with sliding movements or pulling the strings to produce microtonal inflections. The *vīnā* is equipped with seven metal strings: four for melodic work (although it is common for the melody to be concentrated on the uppermost of these) and three for the occasional emphasis of metrically-important moments in the music. The strings are normally set to produce alternately the first and fifth degrees of the mode in question.

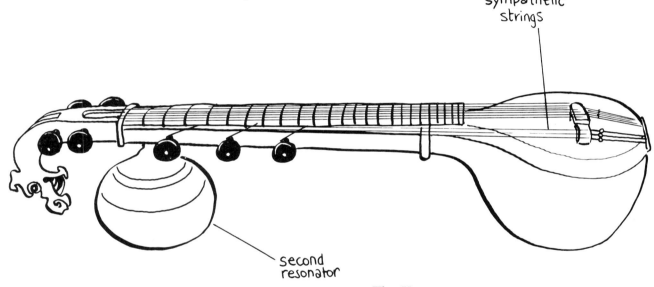

The *Vīnā*

The *vīnā* is accompanied by a *mrdangam* two-headed barrel drum. The *mrdangam* is carefully tuned so that its player can produce a variety of different pitches in support of the melody instrument. Most often, it is pitched to match either the tonic or the fifth degree of the *rāga* being performed by the melody instrument.

Rāga

The term *rāga* has been defined as 'mode', as 'melody' and as both of these together. Knowledge of a *rāga* equips the performer with a specific set of pitches arranged into a hierarchy: the musician understands which notes to use, and which ones can begin or end a phrase. Also, experience of a *rāga* provides the musician with typical patterns to use in rising and falling passages, certain points at which ornamentation may be inserted (and possibly which kinds of ornamentation to use at these points) and perhaps a set of key phrases or patterns which can be used to build up a performance. In many cases, the performance of a *rāga* is also linked to an emotional mood and to a particular time, whether a period of the day or a whole season.

 *Track 19*

Varnam

The recorded extract features the *rāga bhairavī*, and is the start of a South Indian musical form called *varnam*. Known since at least the mid-eighteenth century, the *varnam* is a sectional piece which opens a recital of art music. This example begins, quite typically, with a free-time passage performed without drum accompaniment. This is followed by a metrical passage (only partially transcribed). The free-time passage introduces some of the melodic and modal characteristics of the *rāga bhairavī*. Reiteration of the notes e', b and e (the tonic and fifth degrees of this mode) is given to the three rhythm strings of the *vīnā*. This accompanies an improvisatory melody which gradually moves from the exploration of the note b and its neighbours to cover nearly a two-octave range, from high f♯' to low A before ending on the fundamental pitch. In this *rāga* the pitch C♯ is preferred in the lower octave while C natural is usual in the upper octave, and the pitches D and G are relatively little used. Melodic movement is generally by step or small leap, with an undulating contour, ornamented by left-hand sliding and pulling techniques. The melody is more deliberate in the second section, and rhythmically more regular as well. After a short introduction a 28-beat passage, the main theme of the *varnam*, is then played twice with *mrdangam* accompaniment.

Music for *Nāgasvaram*

Cultural background

Solo instrumental recitals (see India: Music for *Vīnā*) are relatively recent occurrences in the field of Indian art music, where for a long time the principal performers were vocalists. Indeed, the Indian term *sangīta*, usually taken as equivalent to the English word 'music', literally means 'concerted song', which again hints at the primacy of the voice among Indian conceptions of this art. Instrumentalists' main role was to provide accompaniment to these singers. However, beyond the confines of the art music world, many instrument-centred traditions exist, one of which is *nāgasvaram*, a genre of temple ceremonial music from South India.

Several different styles of musical activity are found in South Indian temples, but *nāgasvaram* is unusual in that it is played by an ensemble of wind and percussion instruments. Until quite recently in many temples, several times each day, such an ensemble performed a *rāga* corresponding to the time of day and ceremony in question, their strong and auspicious sound being thought to create an appropriate mood for worship. A parallel could perhaps be made with the use of organ chorale-preludes in some Western churches. The *nāgasvaram* ensemble also does duty at communal festivities such as weddings and religious processions, and there are now a small number of performers who broadcast on radio and play in concerts.

The *nāgasvaram*

The principal instrument of the ensemble is the double reed *nāgasvaram* – the name of this instrument also serves as the name of the group as a whole. The *nāgasvaram* consists of a fairly long, conical wooden tube, capped at one end with a metal horn, and played through a sizeable reed. There are typically seven finger-holes, as well as a number of other holes, optionally plugged with wax to fine-tune the instrument to the notes of one *rāga* or another. Standard fingering techniques include 'half-holing' to produce pitch slides or otherwise unavailable pitches, and a good performer also needs to learn great flexibility of embouchure and lip pressure.

On the recording, the solo *nāgasvaram* is accompanied by two further *nāgasvaram* which supply drone notes and imitative phrases. Drones are also produced by a *sruti* box, effectively a small harmonium capable of playing just a handful of pitches at any one time. Rhythmic emphasis is provided by the *tāvil* two-headed barrel drum. This is played by sounding the more tense (higher-pitched) head with the wrist and fingers (perhaps protected by caps) and the slacker (lower-pitched) head with a stick. Strikes of the *tālam* small bronze cymbals mark the main beats of each rhythmic cycle.

Tempo and metre

In North Indian classical music it is possible for a performer gradually to increase musical tempo whilst remaining in the same metre. This is not the case in *nāgasvaram* music, where it is more usual for a composition to begin slowly, then abruptly shift to double speed, and possibly double in tempo once or twice more as the performance continues. As a result, the latter sections of a musical performance can become very dense in rhythmic terms.

Listeners (and singers) habitually keep track of the metre of a performance through a system of hand gestures. Main beats are marked with a clap of the hands, while subsidiary beats are counted out with the thumb on the fingers of the right hand or shown with a wave of the whole hand. The recorded example uses a common metrical structure of South Indian music called *ādi tāla*, which consists of an eight-beat cycle, subdivided into groups of four, two and two. Hand movements for this cycle are as shown below. The main beats (1, 5 and 7) are theoretically reinforced by the sounding of the *tālam* cymbals, although in section 1 of the recorded example only beats 1 and 5 are marked in this way; later on, when the tempo is doubled in section 2, beats 1, 5, 6, 7 and 8 are all articulated by the *tālam*.

Beat	1	2	3	4	5	6	7	8
Gesture	clap	little finger touch	ring finger touch	middle finger touch	clap	wave	clap	wave

Pattern of Hand Movements in *Ādi Tāla*

 *Track 20*

Dudukulu Gaula

The performance from which an excerpt has been transcribed is a rendition of a composition by a prominent South Indian musician of the past, Tyagaraja (1767–1847). It uses the *rāga gaula*, which consists in its most fundamental form of an ascending pentatonic note-set (broadly equivalent to D, E♭, G, A, C in this case) and descending hexatonic set (D, C, A, G, F♯, E♭, D). D is the tonic note, and is present throughout as a drone, together with the pitch A. These two are also the most important notes in the melody, being used to begin and end many phrases. As mentioned already, the subsidiary *nāgasvaram* play drone notes and imitative phrases following the patterns of the soloist. However, all three occasionally play in unison, for instance at the opening of section 2. This variation of texture makes the music more interesting for the listener.

General rhythmic and metrical characteristics of this piece have been discussed above, but particularly noteworthy is the change in drum-style from the spare patterns of the first section to the much denser ostinato of the second. The drum has a structural role too. Apart from providing a prelude before section 1 (not transcribed), the drum also connects the two sections with a passage of more elaborate rhythmic work.

Music for *Pakhāvaj*

Cultural background

The *pakhāvaj* is a form of drum widely used in North India, and is related to the *mrdangam* of the south. It is an old instrument, and is predominantly found today in performances of the longer-established North Indian forms, such as the song style *dhrupad*. Today, the *pakhāvaj* is played both in religious contexts and in secular concerts, and has both accompanimental and solo roles. Both these performance contexts are quite formal, and conservative with regard to the adoption of new styles of performance or new instruments, so the *pakhāvaj* has not been replaced by the more recently invented pair of drums found in much other North Indian music, the *tablā*. However, while formal performance contexts help preserve older instruments and musical styles, they also encourage specialism and inventiveness on the part of composers and performers. This is illustrated by the recorded extract, which demonstrates a contemporary musician's rendition of a complex rhythmic cycle more usually found only in historical treatises. In order to bring the music to life, the drummer has composed an accompaniment melody and devised a rhythmic ostinato for the bell.

Another interesting aspect of this tradition is its use of what some refer to as 'oral notation'. Drummers learn to chant, often with great virtuosity, special syllables, each of which is associated with a particular drum stroke or beat of the music. Of course, these syllables are sometimes written down, but, in the past, this was not a standard part of the composing, learning or performing process.

Instrumentation

On the recorded extract, the principal instrument is the two-headed, wooden *pakhāvaj* barrel-drum. This drum is played with the hands, and, like several other Indian forms of drum, has one high-pitched and one lower-pitched head. Several layers of black tuning paste are applied to the centre of the right-hand, higher-pitched head, giving the player a choice of three areas to strike: the edge of the drum, the ring of skin and the central circle of paste. Each area produces a different timbre. Timbre can be further varied by use of different striking techniques or by stopping the head immediately upon striking it. The left-hand head is also coated with a substance, in this case a mixture of dough which lowers its pitch to approximately an octave below that of the other head. The player sits to perform, the drum resting laterally on a cloth before him.

 *Track 21*

Ganesh Paran

In the transcribed extract, the soloist first performs an invocation (section 1) which combines the chanting of traditional drum syllables with other text, predominantly the various names of Ganesh Paran, a god who clears obstacles – appropriate for opening a recital. Other syllables heard include 'Laksmītāla', the name of the rhythmic cycle employed as the music progresses. The soloist then repeats the whole passage (section 2), this time performing the syllables on the *pakhāvaj*, imitating the sounds of the sacred names and other words with appropriate drum sounds.

Section 3 introduces *laksmītāla*, which is an eighteen-beat cycle subdivided into groups of 2+1+1+2+1+1+2+1+1+1+1+1+1+1+1. Since this cycle is presumed unfamiliar to many of his listeners, the soloist has added a rhythmic ostinato for *ghanti* bell and a cyclic melody (as noted above) played heterophonically by the harmonium and long-necked lute *surbahar*. To each repetition of the melody, which is based on the *rāga darbārī kānadā*, the soloist fits a different set of drum rhythms. Those heard in the first three cycles are relatively straightforward, but as the performance progresses much more elaborate patterns are incorporated. Also, the tempo is gradually increased, further challenging the technique of the drummer.

Looking more closely at the drum syllables transcribed in sections 1 and 3, and comparing them to their sound as performed on the *pakhāvaj*, it can be seen that the syllables are largely phonetic, imitating the sound of the respective drum strokes. Thus, strokes on the higher-pitched head are normally shown by a syllable beginning with a clearly-articulated 't' sound. Strokes on the lower-pitched face are begun with a less abrupt 'g' sound, while syllables representing simultaneous strokes on both drum-heads are given a moderate 'd' beginning. Longer vowel sounds tend to be used for the more resonant strokes, and damped strokes are likely to be represented with a syllable completed by a consonant, perhaps 't' for a dry, staccato sound or 'n' for a sustained but muffled sound. Although these syllables can be employed individually by a composer working out a new piece, some of them are typically found in combination. For instance, the stroke represented by 'ki' is often followed immediately by a 'ta' stroke. A longer example occurs at the end of section 1, where a three-beat pattern beginning 'ta-gi-na-dhā' is heard three times (the final beat overlaps with the first beat of section 2, and has not been transcribed).

Iran

Art Music for Ensemble

Cultural background

Iran, formerly Persia, has a rich musical heritage, incorporating important historical treatises dealing with musical theory and instruments, the folk traditions of different regions and ethnic groups, and a private art music style as well as more recently adopted Westernized forms. Sufi musicians were important in the maintenance of Persian art music, and many songs set Sufi poems. Important elements of this art music were adopted by Arabs and other Islamic peoples, and spread by them to South and Central Asia, throughout the Middle East and into the Southern Mediterranean, Turkey and the Balkans. Nonetheless, over the last four centuries and particularly since the 1980s, the increasing influence of Shiite Muslim beliefs has strongly discouraged the performance of some styles. There is concern that these will now be lost, since although music notation existed in Persia for over one thousand years, it was never widely used in the transmission of music. Instead, apprentice musicians learnt their repertories and performance techniques entirely by rote. Thus, music not actively maintained in performance can be forgotten within a few generations.

Dastgāh

Persian art music is typically described as falling into twelve systems, called *dastgāh*, literally 'hand positions' but more often translated as 'scheme', 'organization' or 'system'. Arising at some point in the last two centuries, a *dastgāh* is both the title of a set of pieces which may pass through several different modes, and also the identification of the specific mode used in the first piece of this set. Each *dastgāh* includes pre-composed pieces and passages of improvisation based on the modes used within the set. However, a clear distinction between composition and improvisation is not acknowledged by traditional Persian musicians, who see themselves as essentially the performers of pre-existent music, whether or not that music already exists in an entirely fixed form.

In performance, a *dastgāh* begins with an introductory section which establishes the mode (*maqām*) and presents the primary melodic patterns of that *dastgāh*. Following the introduction, further sections (*gusheh-hā*, singular *gusheh*) generally move to new tonal areas. Some shift higher or lower in register. Others remain in the opening register but alter the melodic emphasis among the notes selected or replace one or two notes with new ones. All of these changes are forms of modulation. In order to bind the *gusheh-hā* into a set, they often end with a common cadential formula which reasserts the opening mode and melodic patterns.

Many *gusheh-hā* have a total range of a fourth or fifth. Thus, musicians normally play them in sequence, each section moving a note or two higher than the previous one. Because each section of a *dastgāh* relies primarily on a narrow register, Persian musicians tend to prefer not to explain their music in terms of scales stretching over the range of an octave.

Tasnif

Traditional *dastgāh* music was played solo, and involved an amount of rhythmic and melodic freedom as the performer worked out the details of the mode, modulations and melodic patterns selected. Following the introduction of Western music, some early twentieth-century Persian musicians devised more fixed forms in which several instrumentalists could play together. These forms can be played together with a *dastgāh*, and may draw their melodic material from it, but they normally have a regular metrical structure and fixed pattern of phrases.

One example is the *tasnif*, originally a form of ballad but now often placed at the end of a *dastgāh* and sung to a metrical instrumental ensemble accompaniment. Learnt by rote, the *tasnif* uses the same mode as the *dastgāh* it completes, though some include modulations of the kinds discussed above. During the 1920s and '30s the composer Ali Naqi Vaziri added an instrumental introduction to the *tasnif*, inserting ensemble passages between each verse of text as well. More recently, some musicians have added harmonized accompaniments.

 *Track 22*

Tasnif Djān-e Djahān

The *tasnif* transcribed is more typical of those produced earlier this century. There is an extensive instrumental introduction in simple triple time performed by a heterophonic ensemble of *ney* end-blown flute, *santur* dulcimer, *ud* lute, *tār* long-necked lute and *kamānche* spike fiddle. Most phrases remain within the range of a fourth or fifth. The simple triple metre of the ballad is maintained throughout by a rhythmic ostinato performed on the *daf* frame drum and *zarb* goblet-shaped drum. In some passages this ostinato is also doubled by some of the lower-pitched melodic instruments.

This *tasnif* is set in the *dastgāh navā*, which can be explained as a heptatonic scale covering the range D, E♭ (this sign is a *koron*, or quartertone flat), F, G, A, B♭, C. G is considered the melodic centre and final cadence note in this modal scheme, but F and E are important also. As discussed above, a single section of this *dastgāh* is unlikely to use all seven notes at once. Nonetheless, the instrumental introduction transcribed shows the whole range, though not in a single phrase; this reflects the looser organization of the *tasnif*.

The instrumental introduction recorded is formed from a series of repeated phrases which cadence to F, G, E, G and E respectively. The opening line of the vocal entry returns to the original cadence on F, and is then repeated by the instruments alone. The pattern of short vocal phrases echoed by the melodic instruments while moving gradually through different parts of the register is continued through the rest of the *tasnif*.

Taksim for *Ney*

Cultural background

Turkish music falls into a diverse series of categories, ranging from art music closely related to that of other Near Eastern peoples to regional folk songs, dances and instrumental ensembles and to a thriving tradition of popular song known as *arabesk*. Since the 1920s, the Turkish state has encouraged musicians to create modernized forms of older art and folk musics, often drawing on Western techniques and characteristics. Musical styles have also been developed in Turkey by various Islamic sects, most notably the Dervishes, and Western art and popular music are well known there. Conversely, the influence of Turkish musical forms has been felt across Eastern Europe, throughout the Mediterranean and in the Near East.

Turkish Sufi music

Numerous Sufi Orders and Brotherhoods are musically active in Islamic areas. In distinction to more orthodox groups who seek to distance music and religion (see Egypt: Quran Recitation), music is an integral part of Sufi worship. Among the several Turkish Sufi groups, one of the most prominent is the Mevlevî Order, founded in the thirteenth century and renowned for their characteristic whirling dance. The Mevlevî Order achieved considerable influence during the period of the Ottoman Empire when Mevlevî musicians sustained the court art music tradition, but has declined since the foundation of a secular Turkish republic in the early twentieth century. Because of this historical role, their instrumental music is closely related to the classical art music of secular groups.

Mevlevî music includes instrumental music for an ensemble of *ney* flute and *kudüm* drum. These instruments also accompany songs and hymns, to which dancing takes place. The *ney* is a long, end-blown flute made of reed-cane. It is held at a slightly oblique angle during performance. Varieties of *ney* are found across the Middle East, where it is the only wind instrument commonly used to perform art music. The *kudüm* is a pair of small kettledrums. The right-hand drum is lower in pitch, and is struck on strong beats, while the higher-pitched, left-hand drum is struck on auxiliary beats. Sacred song texts are often derived from mystic poetry, and this music and dance is believed to help its listeners and practitioners achieve ecstatic union with Allah.

Makam* and *usul

Makam (Arabic *maqām*) is the Turkish word for a scale, and the associated melodic guidelines used in the composition and performance of art music using that particular scale. Several hundred of these are possible, but Turkish musicians recognize thirteen as fundamental. Within each *makam*, melodic guidelines govern the relative importance of each pitch, the range available, and melodic rise and fall. Although some compositions are memorized in fixed form, it is also common for musicians to improvise creatively using the rules of the *makam*.

Usul refers to the specific metrical structure underpinning a melodic composition. Turkish music includes simple and elaborate metrical patterns, with and without syncopation. While many pieces are based on the repetition of a symmetrical pattern of 2, 3 or 4 drum beats, some employ much longer models or rely on rhythms of 5, 7 or 11 beats. Others divide a regular number of beats into asymmetrical units. An 8-beat pattern may be composed of units of 3+3+2, while a 9-beat pattern may subdivide into 2+2+2+3. In dance music, units of 3 may be explained as 'long' steps and those of 2 as 'short' steps. In some performances drum accompaniments are omitted, but the soloist or ensemble is still likely to stick to a single *usul* throughout. Nonetheless, the actual rhythmic patterns of the melodic part can be quite independent from the underlying rhythmic framework.

 *Track 23*

Taksim Hüseyni

The music recorded is an improvisation for solo *ney* accompanied by *kudüm*. The term for an improvisation of this kind is *taksim* (Arabic *taqsīm*). A *taksim* is often performed as a prelude to a longer instrumental piece or song. In the *taksim* the performer gradually works through the melodic characteristics and range of the *makam*, which will be featured more fully in the following composition. As such, the improvisation is through-composed, although some melodic patterns recur transformed; compare for example bars 16–28 with 50–58 or bars 38–39 with bar 71. A *taksim* need not follow a single *usul* throughout, but this example does, the *kudüm* player varying a simple, duple-metre pattern.

This *taksim* uses the *hüseyni* mode. In this mode A is the fundamental note, with E functioning as the dominant. The pitches D and G are also important, the former being used to end several phrases and the latter twice sustained for several bars. Other notes in this heptatonic mode are B, which is one comma flat (about an eighth of a tone), C and F♯. There are also occasional chromatic passages during this performance where the performer slides from one pitch to another. In all, the *taksim* ranges over an eleventh, from low g' to high c''', but most of the melody takes place within the octave a'–a'', clustering within the upper part of this octave. Melodic movement is most often by step.

Egypt

Quran Recitation

Cultural background Recitation of the Quran is not considered musical performance by its habitual practitioners. Instead, Muslims classify the chanting of scriptures as a style of performance similar to the recitation of classical poetry. The concept of 'music' in Muslim societies refers principally to instrumental styles commonly used to accompany singing and dancing. To describe Quran recitation, which has no instrumental accompaniment, as 'musical' would therefore connect the sober presentation of holy texts with frivolous forms of entertainment. Thus, when Western listeners study Quran recitation as a form of Islamic religious music, they impose their own, broader and more positive-value definition of music upon this performance art. Accordingly, the results of such study will be more useful to the Western listener than to the Quran-reciters themselves.

Quran recitation According to historical records, concert-style Quran recitations occurred as long ago as the mid-seventh century. However, these were criticized by those who believed the religious content was cheapened by secular performance, and since the twelfth century they have been much less common. There are, however, schools for Quran recitation, and also international contests where it can be heard outside the normal context. Today, Egypt is considered a centre of Quran recitation, and some Egyptian reciters, such as al-Shaik 'Abd al-Bast 'Abd al-Samad, are well known throughout the Islamic world.

This is not deemed a musical activity, so there are no set rules on melodic style other than the avoidance of popular tunes and the insistence that the Arabic text is important, not the tune. Therefore, a good recitalist uses melodic patterns which aid comprehension of the text. Some syllables are sung melismatically (with more than one pitch to each syllable) but most receive a single, steady note. The performer uses some grace notes, trills and vibrato to decorate the recitation, as well as occasional vocal slides between one note and another. Certain vowel and consonant sounds are emphasized, in accordance with rules for pronunciation and intonation.

In performing these words, the reciters use written texts but no musical notation, so many different regional styles of performance have developed. In some of these, reciters adopt or adapt features of Arabic art music, using one of the modes (*maqāmat*) and its associated melodic and ornamental styles, possibly modulating from one mode to another during a reading.

Structure

Whilst there are variations in style from one region, school of singing or individual to another, much Quran recitation shares certain general features. Firstly, each chapter (*sūrat*) is divided into phrases. Phrases are primarily musical units, in that each can set part of a verse of text, although phrases which coincide with complete verses are more common. The longest chapter of the Quran has 286 verses, the shortest just a handful, so the length of a recitation is quite variable. A second general structural feature is that each phrase is separated by an extensive period of silence, perhaps as long in duration as the musical phrase which preceded it. Thirdly, at the opening of the recitation the recitalist warms up his voice in a relatively low register. Gradually, the performer pushes higher, perhaps rising to a register as much as an octave above where he began. The remainder of the recitation takes place within that register, except that there are periodic returns to the lower octave for a line or two. This structures the recitation for the listener and also permits the performer to relax his vocal chords, at least temporarily.

Track 24

Sūrat Yusūf

The *sūrat* partially recorded and transcribed is from a complete performance lasting more than thirty minutes. The text tells the story of Joseph (Yusūf), who is thrown into a pit by his jealous brothers, taken to Egypt, becomes renowned for his ability to interpret dreams, and is eventually reunited with his brothers and father.

Typically, the *sūrat* opens with the words 'A'ūdu billāhi ...', meaning 'God is my refuge', and another standard opening phrase, 'In the name of God, the Compassionate, the Merciful.' Phrase 3 sets three letters, 'Alif Lam Ra' ', the significance of which is not understood today. There follow four further introductory verses, which inform listeners that the words they will hear come from the Quran, and are revealed in narrative form in order to increase their understanding of the message contained within the text. Only then does the story itself begin. The transcription records this introductory material:

Phrase	Comments
1	low-pitched; level contour fluctuating between B♭ and C
2	begins ascent; moves up to E♭ before settling on C
3	slightly higher overall; level contour (D♭); short final syllable
4	restarts ascent; rises to E♭ before returning to C; extended in duration
5	continues ascent; rises fleetingly to G♭ before falling to C; more extended
6	continues ascent; pushes up to G♮ before decorated cadence in higher register
7	continues ascent; reaches A♭ before similar decorated cadence

Taqsīm for Arghūl

Cultural background

Many relics from Egypt's extensive history have survived, including musical instruments. Others are depicted in sculptures and paintings, which suggest how and when instruments were played, though not what they sounded like. About thirteen centuries ago, Islamic Arabs conquered Egypt, introducing their own culture and musical preferences. Today Islam remains important, and Egyptian art music shares many characteristics with the classical musical traditions of other Muslim countries. However, rural folk music retains a contrasting style and instrumentation in each region of Egypt.

Since the advent of Islam, instrumental music, through its association with entertainment and the dangers of sensory over-indulgence, has held an ambiguous position in Egyptian society (see Egypt: Quran Recitation). Certain religious leaders have condemned instrumental music. On the other hand, many Egyptians enjoy this music and would not dispense with it altogether. As a result, professional musicians, perhaps the descendants of slaves and foreigners, have often formed a caste slightly apart from the rest of Islamic society. Although useful to society, the social position of these professionals has traditionally been low. Amateur performers who play for personal interest rather than financial gain or group socialization are generally more highly regarded than paid specialists or ensemble players. Individuality is emphasized in performance by the development of improvisatory skills.

The *arghūl*

The *arghūl*, a cane double clarinet, may be a very old instrument indeed; similar-looking instruments appear on Old Kingdom illustrations from over four thousand years ago. However, cane does not easily survive such lengths of time, and no actual specimens from this period have been discovered so far. The Arabic word *arghūl*, perhaps from 'organ', dates from the later Middle Ages. Today, the *arghūl* is primarily a folk instrument played at wedding dances, to accompany folk singing and for leisure.

There are three different-sized models of *arghūl*. Each consists of two cylindrical tubes headed by a single reed encased in a tubular mouthpiece. The melody pipe is the shorter of the two, and is pierced by five or six finger-holes. The longer drone pipe is generally extended by the insertion of up to three additional segments, giving a combined length of as much as 2.5 metres. Removing one or two of the extensions raises the pitch of the drone. The drone pitch chosen is normally the fundamental of the mode in which the musician wishes to play. Instruments with six finger-holes can play diatonic melodies up to an octave in range, with cross-fingerings producing chromatic pitches. By partially covering certain holes, microtonal adjustments can be made. Performers must also master circular breathing, i.e. puffing air held in the cheeks through the instrument to sustain the sound whilst inhaling through the nostrils.

Maqām

The usual translation of *maqām* is 'mode', but a *maqām* is more than simply a hierarchy of pitches arranged in a scale. Each *maqām* is further characterized by the use of certain typical melodic shapes, frequently-employed motifs and customary ornamental patterns. Finally, each *maqām* is associated with a particular mood or emotion. Knowledge of a *maqām* guides the musician in the act of improvisation since it identifies a mood, a set of notes, a collection of set phrases and patterns, and provides standardized ways of interpreting them.

Taqsīm

Taqsīm, or 'division', refers to a form of instrumental music in which a soloist improvises on the characteristic melodic contour and motifs of a given mode. Sometimes, the instrumentalist modulates away from the opening mode to visit others, returning periodically to the original. Generally, a *taqsīm* is unmetred, though it will contain patterns of stresses and long and short notes, possibly originally inspired by the reading manner of Middle Eastern poetry. Sometimes metred sections are inserted, with one or two percussion instruments providing rhythmic support. It is also possible for another musician to accompany the soloist on a second melody instrument, either playing in unison during metred sections and echoing the soloist a note or two behind in the freer parts, or providing a drone with occasional melodic echoes. Often used to open musical occasions, a *taqsīm* can last between one minute and quarter of an hour, depending on the skill of the soloist and the receptivity of the audience.

 *Track 25*

Taqsīm for *arghūl*

The excerpt transcribed is a relatively short performance of an unmetred improvisatory *taqsīm*, which was followed by a short, ternary-form dance in simple duple time (not shown on the transcription). The *arghūl* used is one of the smallest, its drone pipe set to the pitch B. A range of one octave is used, beginning with a seven-note (heptatonic) mode similar to the Western diatonic major scale in its arrangement of tones and semitones. Particularly important in this first section are the pitches B and F♯, with D♯ playing a subsidiary role. Modulation to a different *maqām* takes place as the tempo temporarily drops and the pitch A replaces A♯ (amongst other alterations). Emphasis also moves away from the pitches B and F♯. Later, other pitches, for example E♯, are introduced as further modal excursions take place. The soloist also begins to use slides, slowly moving a finger across a finger-hole to ensure a smooth pitch change. Other finger ornamentations employed are mordents and trills.

The *taqsīm* also demonstrates how phrases are improvised from short motifs of just a few notes. These motifs may then be further developed as in the illustration below. Other motifs are treated sequentially, the same pattern being repeated at a higher or lower pitch.

Motivic Development in an Egyptian *Taqsīm*

Music for Folk Ensemble

Cultural background

Sometimes, professional folk musicians are hired to perform instrumental solos, dances and songs at traditional wedding celebrations in Upper Egypt. The Western art music concept of the carefully notated, original musical work, identically recreated during each performance, is one foreign to the majority of traditional musical styles world-wide. Instead, many folk musicians, such as those of Upper Egypt, re-use tunes they already know, adapting them during performance in ways appropriate to the context and function of the occasion. For example, in the case of a wedding, the principal vocalist may adjust a memorized song text, improvising phrases complimenting the guests, in return for which the guests will be expected to respond with gifts of money. Large-scale pieces, rather than being memorized as such, may be more informally created during performance by combining shorter items: pre-composed songs, instrumental music and passages of improvisation.

Instrumentation

The composition recorded and transcribed is performed by an ensemble of six musicians. The leader plays the *rabāba* two-stringed spike fiddle, as do two of his subordinates. A fourth musician performs the obliquely-held *suffāra* cane flute. The other members of the group are percussionists, one performing the *duff* frame drum, and one the *darabukka* goblet drum. The leader also takes a principal role in singing, the other musicians responding as a chorus. In general, the melodic instruments perform in heterophonic style, simultaneously producing individually decorated versions of a common melody. In some instances, the bowed instruments also support a solo with a drone bass, or imitate the contour of the vocalist's phrases. Occasionally, a musician will improvise a more independent melodic line (as in the *suffāra* part transcribed in section 5).

The *rabāba* (plural *rabāb*) is often made from a hollowed-out coconut shell faced with fish-skin. This resonator is transfixed by a long, tubular handle. Two tuning pegs are inserted at the top, one for each horse-hair string. These are usually tuned a fourth or fifth apart. At the base of the handle is an iron spike, which rests on the left leg during performance.

In Egypt *suffāra* is a generic term for flute. The Egyptian *suffāra* is made from reed, though wood and metal instruments are also found. Six finger-holes are drilled in the tube, some instruments having an additional thumb-hole. The player blows obliquely across the rim at the tube's upper end. A skilled player can produce a range of two and a half octaves, though this is not required in all traditional ensemble pieces.

The *duff* consists of a sheet of skin stretched over a wooden frame. Often, though not in this case, it is fitted with jingles, making it similar to a tambourine. The *darabukka* is an important instrumental type in Middle Eastern music, consisting of a pottery, clay or wooden goblet-shaped vessel faced with skin. The performer's right hand strikes the *darabukka* forcefully towards the centre of the skin, while the left-hand fingers beat more gently at the rim. Some performers press with one hand whilst striking with the other, a technique which raises the drum's pitch. In performance, the *darabukka* is either tucked under the left arm and supported by the musician's leg or placed on the ground.

The *Darabukka*

Track 26

Yā Farawla

This composite piece, 'Oh Strawberry', is named after one of the songs it incorporates, where the leading singer likens the rouged cheeks of his beloved to the colour and shape of a strawberry (*farawla*). A hexatonic *maqām* (see Egypt: *Taqsim* for *Arghūl*) is used: B, C♯, D♯ (quartertone sharp), E, F♯, G, A. Structurally, *Yā Farawla* combines sections of improvisation with verses of popular dance and song tunes and poetic recitation. The transcription and recording are only of section 5 and the beginning of section 6, but a brief description of the complete piece will show how these sections fit in context:

Section 1 is begun by the two percussionists. Over an ostinato *duff* rhythm and *darabukka* improvisations, the melodic instruments join in with a popular theme performed in heterophonic style. Section 2 is an unmetred passage begun by a solo improvisation on the *suffāra*, supported by a string drone. The lead singer responds to the *suffāra* melody with recitative-style lament phrases. Finally there are free melodic echoes of these vocal phrases by the *rabāba* and *suffāra*. Section 3 is a short, fast, metred passage for the whole instrumental ensemble. Section 4 is akin in some respects to section 2, featuring vocal recitative-style calls answered by instrumental echoes, though now the song text moves on to describe the singer's beloved in a loosely poetic style. The latter part of this section is punctuated by sporadic drum beats, which provide a link into the following section.

Section 5 (transcribed) recalls the style of the opening, the same rhythmic ostinato reappearing in the *duff*. Again, there is a percussion introduction (bars 78–79) followed by an instrumental rendition of a popular theme (bars 80–95). This time, however, the musicians sing when the verse is repeated, first led by the soloist and then by the chorus (bars 96–112). During the repeats, the *suffāra* player improvises a more independent melodic line.

Section 6 (partially transcribed) alternates four-bar phrases for leader and chorus over a melodic and percussive accompaniment which continues in the style of the previous section, i.e. ostinato *duff* patterns, faster, varying rhythms on the *darabukka* and primarily heterophonic *rabāba* and *suffāra* lines. Section 7 brings the vocal solo calls and group responses even closer, now occurring at intervals of one bar. Section 8 acts as a reprise, and a few phrases of chorus chants complete this section. Once it has been repeated, the ensemble works its way through sections 6–8 twice more.

As can be appreciated, there is a great deal of variety (metrical, timbral, rhythmic, tempo, texture) in this sectional structure. Nonetheless, overall consistency results from use of a common mode, related melodic material and similar rhythmic patterns, and from the repetition of earlier sections.

Morocco

Nawba **Music for Ensemble**

Cultural background

Moroccan musical traditions combine indigenous features with aspects of art and folk music styles from Europe, the Middle East and North and West Africa. For example, classical 'Andalusian music' is claimed to have been imported from Europe in the late fifteenth century by Muslims forced from Spain. More recent European influence has also transformed the instrumentation of this music (see below). Closely related traditions occur in Tunisia and Algeria, and, more distantly, in Egypt, Syria and elsewhere. The musicians who specialize in this music are often members of religious Sufi brotherhoods.

The Sufi connection may explain the association of the different modes of Andalusian music with Moroccan cosmology. Each mode is also related to a particular time of day, that recorded being an evening mode. Apparently, each mode promotes a specific humour or temperament in the listener; thus, musical performance becomes a means of therapy.

Andalusian music

Andalusian music consists of about a dozen suites of instrumental and song sections. Each suite, or *nawba*, relies on a single mode, variety resulting from the contrasting metres of each section and from a gradual movement from slow to fast songs within each section. Unmetred passages are found also, both at the very beginning of the *nawba* and amongst the songs themselves. Songs are preceded by instrumental introductions, and interludes separate most songs. A full *nawba*, lasting several hours, includes five sections in different metres, each section containing several songs at each speed. Today, shortened versions are more usual.

Instrumentation

Andalusian music is performed by an ensemble of stringed instruments, percussion and male voices, the instrumentalists doubling as singers. One singer, who specializes in solo, melismatic passages, does not play an instrument; his voice is considered part of the instrumental ensemble. The leader of the ensemble typically plays the *rabāb*, a vertically-held fiddle with two strings and a short, arched bow. Today, a violin and two or three violas may be played also; these may follow an older European design, being positioned vertically on the lap. Some contemporary ensembles add cello and piano. Two musicians play the pear-shaped lute *'ūd*. Percussion instruments include the *tār* tambourine, *darabukka* single-headed ceramic drum and *tbilāt* ceramic kettledrums.

The ensemble recorded has attempted to reconstruct an instrumental combination typical of the eighteenth century. Of the recent European instruments, they have kept only a single viola strung with old-style gut strings. Moroccan instruments used are the *rabāb*, *'ūd*, *suissen* long-necked, three-stringed lute (discarded earlier this century) and *tār*.

① *Track 27*

Nawba hijāzī al-kabīr

The mode from which this suite takes its name, *hijāzī al-kabīr*, is a heptatonic mode consisting of D, E♭ (a quartertone flat), F♯ (sometimes altered to F♮), G, A, B and C. D and G are the main cadence notes, but some phrases end on A and E. Most of the suite is pre-composed and memorized, but some details are left to the musicians' discretion during performance, for example occasional improvised passages of melismatic song echoed by solo instruments in turn. Improvisation is supported by the fact that music notation is not employed, although song texts, which date back to the court poetry of Muslim Spain, are written down. Generally, performance is heterophonic, but improvisatory passages are more likely to use antiphonal or drone textures.

The instrumental introduction has been partially transcribed. This has two parts, the first unmetred and the second metrical. The opening part (Section **A** and its varied repeat **A'**), consists of a series of phrases in which melodic movement is mainly by step. These outline the mode to be used in the remainder of the suite. The second part (Sections **B** and **C**, both repeated) again concentrates on stepwise motion but sets it in a regular metrical framework. The second part is analysed below. The transcription shows Sections **A'** to **C** (first hearing).

Section	Phrase	Length	Comments on New Material
B	a	12 beats	begins with unison dotted rhythm on D, rises to A, then falls to low G cadence
	b	8 beats	same cadence note but opposite melodic contour; falls to A, rises to G cadence
	x	3 beats	link leading down towards D for repeat of **a**
	a	12 beats	
	a'	8 beats	final four-beat segment of phrase **a** repeated twice more in place of b. Note: **a'** has same duration and cadence note as **b** and is also set, like **b**, between **a** and **x**
	x	3 beats	
B	a, b, x, a, a', x	(repeat)	
	a	12 beats	extra phrase **a** rounds off repeat of section **B**
C	d	8 beats	contrasting melody, but still very much in style of **B**. Cadences to low A
	y	4 beats	cadence pattern ending on D
	d	8 beats	
	y'	8 beats	cadence pattern extended
C	d, y, d, y'	(repeat)	

Music for *Ghayta* and *Bendir*

Cultural background

Music in Algeria is related in many respects to that of neighbouring Morocco. There have been similar influences from indigenous Berber and foreign Arabic and Mediterranean cultures. Similar instruments are used in both nations, and music is performed at parallel occasions. In the art music repertory, Algerian musicians perform their own versions of the 'Andalusian music' *nawbāt* suites also found in Morocco. Another shared form of music from this area, one used at weddings and festive occasions in general, is that for oboe and drum. In Algeria it is believed that this combination was first introduced by the invading Ottoman Turks in the fifteenth century.

The combination of an oboe-type instrument with a drum to accompany dancing is one found in many parts of North Africa, in Eastern Europe and across much of Asia. In many of these countries, the form of oboe used is broadly similar. Also, across the whole region, it is common for performers to employ circular breathing. Using the pressure of the puffed cheeks to expel air through the double reed, the musician simultaneously inhales through the nostrils. In this way, it is possible to maintain an unbroken sound on a wind instrument. Despite these similarities, oboe and drum music also varies across this huge area, reflecting local scales, melodies, musical forms and contexts. In Algeria, for instance, oboe and drum music is used in court music and religious festivals as well as to accompany folk dance.

Instrumentation

In Algeria the form of oboe employed is known as the *ghayta*. It has a wooden body punctured by seven finger-holes and one rear thumb-hole. At the base is a flaring bell, into which several sound holes are drilled. At the top, a small double reed is fixed onto a metal staple, or tube. The staple passes through a disc of metal, ivory or wood known as a pirouette. During performance, the musician places the whole reed inside his mouth, resting his lips on the pirouette. Typically, the *ghayta* has a range of about an octave and a half, although in this dance it uses only the range of a seventh. Finger ornamentations – fast trills, turns and grace notes – are an important part of *ghayta* performance style. Sustained pitches can also be elaborated by repeated staccato tonguing.

The *ghayta* is regularly accompanied by the single-headed, circular frame drum *bendir*, although in some areas the goblet drum *darabukka* is added too (see Egypt: Music for Folk Ensemble). The *bendir* consists of a large wooden frame of perhaps 50cm in diameter, over which a goatskin face has been stretched. One or two snares are attached. The *bendir* is held like a tambourine and struck with the right hand during performance.

 *Track 28*

Dance from the Aurès Mountains

The Aurès Mountains are located in southern Algeria on the boundary of the Sahara Desert. Music for *ghayta*, *bendir* and *darabukka* is widely used in this region, particularly at weddings and other celebrations. Normally, a single *ghayta* provides a melody accompanied by a rhythmic ostinato from the drum or drums. In some cases, a second *ghayta* adds a drone pitch throughout the dance, or both play in unison throughout.

The particular dance recorded and transcribed is a fast one in simple duple time for *bendir* and a single *ghayta*. The scale used is a heptatonic series of pitches broadly equivalent to F, G, A♭, B♭, C, D♭ and E. Sometimes G♭ is used for variety.

The final F♭ is probably due to a decrease in breath pressure rather than a change of mode. The melody consists of a series of short phrases and melodic patterns which are spun together. Since the last few notes of one pattern are often used as the first few notes of the next, it is difficult for the listener to say exactly where one phrase ends and the next begins. Nonetheless, it is possible to split the main thematic material into two parts, **A** and **B**.

In theme **A** (bars 1–13) the patterns played in bars 2–7 are especially important, being repeated throughout the piece, often in varied form. Unlike theme **A**, which uses mainly the lower notes of the *ghayta*'s range, theme **B** (bars 14–22) predominantly exploits the upper segment of the register. It also contrasts rhythmically with theme **A**, and features the staccato repeated-note decoration not found in **A**. After these two themes, the material is repeated in developed form as follows (only the next two sections are given in full):

Section	Phrases	=	Based on	Comment (if any)
23–45		**A**		
	23–27	=	3–7	
	28–31	=	8–11	like 2–5
	32–33	=	7	extended by one bar
	34–37	=	2–5	
	38–43	=	2–7	
	44–45	=	2–3	
46–54		**B**		
	46–47	=	16–17	like 14–15
	48–49	=	18–19	
	50–54	=	18–22	
55–77		**A**		
78–84		**B**		
85–93		**A**		
94		**Coda**		

Summary: **A–B–A–B–A–B–A–Coda**

Mali

Griot Song

Cultural background   Located in West Africa, Mali forms a cultural crossroads between the Arab and Arab-influenced nations to the north and Black Africa to the south. Perhaps due to the varied impact of musical styles from these two areas, Malian musical traditions are notably diverse. However, numerous minority groups live amongst the majority Manding (or Malinke) people in Mali, and music is a very good way for smaller groups within a larger society to maintain and assert their special identities. Therefore, Mali's musical riches may result more from its multi-ethnic population than its geographical location. Whichever explanation is true, Mali questions the old cliché that island nations possess the greatest cultural diversity.

Although several of the minority peoples inhabiting Mali have distinct and interesting musical traditions, discussion here concentrates on a single aspect of Manding music: the hereditary professional praise-singers, or griots. Griot is a French translation of the Manding term *jali*, the most prominent representatives of traditional Manding music. Some Manding people consider amateur musicianship a valuable accomplishment, but important events normally require the participation of griots. Traditionally, one or more griots will be present at all significant occasions, including childbirth, circumcision, betrothals, weddings and funerals. At these events the musicians recall the history and legends of the community, recount the personal genealogy and deeds of the individuals or families central to this ceremony, sing praises to their benefactors, and dispense a musical commentary on current affairs.

Typically, a family of griots is attached to the household of a noble or other influential patron, for whom they may act as a spokesman. Many are well-travelled, having journeyed to meet other griots and take part in distant festivals. As a result, griot song melodies are fairly standardized across the whole Manding area, although new texts are often improvised for new occasions.

Instrumentation

The recorded performance features a male vocal soloist answered by a female singer and accompanied by a *balo* xylophone and *kora* harp-lute. Known since the fourteenth century, the *balo* typically has between fifteen and nineteen cane keys set in a wooden frame to give a range of two-and-a-half octaves. Beneath the frame a row of gourds act as resonators. The keys are struck with a pair of rubber-tipped beaters, some performers wearing bells around their wrists to add a percussive edge to the music.

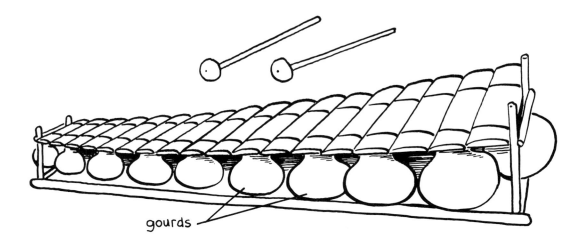

gourds

The *Balo*

The *kora* has a documented history of two hundred years. Its resonator is a large, hemispherical gourd. A fairly long wooden neck is inserted diametrically through the body. The twenty-one strings are stretched in two parallel ranks from the neck over a large bridge, which projects towards the performer, and then back down to the lower end of the neck. A plate is sometimes attached to the bridge, which adds a buzz to its timbre, and a second person may tap a simple rhythm on the body of the instrument to add further rhythmic emphasis.

① *Track 29*

Duga

The basic theme of this song is that of a great warrior named Duga, or 'Vulture', who returns to life after receiving dreadful wounds. Different griots interpret this story in contrasting ways: as a legendary tale about a brave warrior, as a praise song directed to the sacred vulture or as a parable in which the listeners are exhorted to recognize their inherent differences and act accordingly. It is unclear which interpretation the recorded performance favours.

Duga uses a heptatonic scale equivalent to the Western aeolian mode: E, F♯, G, A, B, C, D (transcribed a semitone above the recording). Most melodic phrases end on E, the pitch B being of secondary importance. These two notes, E and B, form the basis of the accompaniment. Two voices perform in antiphonal style (with unison at the very end). Most of the time, the male griot sings the song text in a syllabic style, while the answering female voice supplies melismatic phrases to the vocable 'Ah'. The vocal parts tend toward compound quadruple time and the accompanying heterophonic *kora* and *balo* to simple quadruple time. However, both instrumental and vocal parts are rhythmically flexible, so the music cannot be said to be polymetric. The opening of the song (the passage transcribed) is structured as below:

Bars	Description	Comments
1–9	instrumental introduction	short, melodic phrases alternating with rhythmic reiteration of the notes E (tonic) and B (dominant). Establishes song tempo, metre, melodic style and mode – note how almost every bar opens with E
10–13	first male voice solo	two phrases cadencing to D and E successively. During vocal phrases, instruments mostly reiterate E and B as decorated form of drone accompaniment
14–17	first female voice response	repeats male phrases
18–22	instrumental interlude	based on introduction
22–26	second male solo	lower-register melody contrasting with 10–13, but again cadences to E
26–27	instrumental interlude	as before
27–28	second female response	short vocable passage, little more than stepwise fall to E
28–30	instrumental interlude	as before
30–34	third male solo	higher register, but partially based on earlier material: compare 12–13 with 33–34 Second phrase cadences to E
34–36	third female response	short passage sung to 'Ah', this time beginning on E, falling to low B then leaping up a seventh and working back down to E again
36–38	instrumental interlude	as before
38–42	fourth male solo	varied repeat of 30–34
42–44	fourth female response	repeat of 34–36

Song with *Masenqo*

Cultural background

Modern Ethiopia is culturally diverse, territorial expansion during the nineteenth century having meant that many distinct peoples are now grouped within the nation. Little is known in the West of much Ethiopian music-making, largely because of extended political instability, civil war and resultant famine. Nonetheless – at least among the Amhara people, historically long part of Ethiopia – two cultural strands have proved particularly influential: the continuing impact of African traditions; and that of Christianity, present in Ethiopia since the fourth century.

One particular class of professional Amhara musicians are the *azmaris*, male solo singers who improvise a *masenqo* fiddle accompaniment to their verses. (Sometimes a group perform together, in which case a mixture of instruments will be used). Rather like the Malian griots, the *azmaris* are permitted to say in song what could not be stated in speech. Unlike them, however, they are considered low class (see Mali: Griot Song). Traditionally, the *azmaris* travelled from village to village or court to court to make a living by singing the news or providing entertainment, tailoring their verses and music to the particular occasion. Their verse-style is called 'wax and gold', referring to its use of words with an obvious surface meaning but also a much deeper, internal meaning (the gold hidden within the wax caste) more special or personal to the singer. The transcribed example has a text glorifying Jesus Christ. Here, the overall intention was to entertain a crowd of pilgrims and thereby earn some money, rather than to celebrate a specific religious occasion.

The *masenqo*

The *masenqo* is a one-stringed fiddle with a diamond-shaped soundbox. The neck of the instrument runs diagonally through the body and protrudes at the bottom end. The front and back of the soundbox are leather, which also surrounds the olive-wood sides of the box. The neck of a *masenqo* is about 80cm in length. At its top, a tuning peg controls the tension of the string, which consists of many strands of horsehair. A single bridge stands vertically on the front skin of the soundbox. The bow is an arced piece of wood strung with thick horsehair:

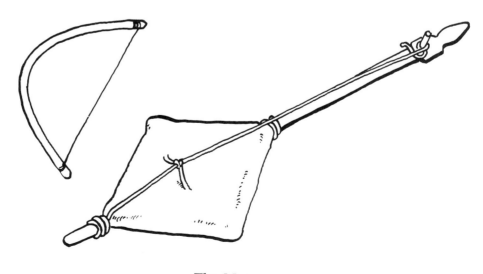

The *Masenqo*

The *masenqo* is played in seated position with the neck reaching towards the player's left shoulder and the soundbox held between the knees. The bow is drawn energetically by the right hand whilst the string is stopped by the fingers and thumb of the left. The use of thumb as well as fingers allows the performer to span quite wide intervals along the length of the string. However, the use of a single fixed-pitch string limits the player to a narrower range than that of a multi-stringed instrument. The exact pitch of the open string is tuned to suit the performer's requirements. The *masenqo* provides an introduction and intermissions to the vocal part it accompanies. Vocal phrases are either accompanied in heterophonic style, as in the transcribed example, or underpinned by an ostinato figure.

 Track 1

Structure

Song with *masenqo*

The whole song consists of many vocal statements, which are introduced by and interspersed with solo passages on the *masenqo*. Similar melodic themes occur throughout the piece; for example the theme of section 2 is mirrored in section 8, and passages 12–14 copy sections 4–6, and we could say that the excerpt has a binary form (sections 1–6 being repeated in decorated form as 7–14). However, the positioning and style of these restatements within the whole song is somewhat irregular, so it may be best to explain the song as having an additive structure. In this kind of form, a performer selects each new passage from a memorized set of vocal phrases and instrumental tunes whilst progressing through the song.

The song is based on a pentatonic scale on Ab: Ab, Bb, C, Eb and F. Db occurs very occasionally as a decoration of either C or Eb. Ab is clearly the tonic note. Most *masenqo* sections end on that note, and vocal lines followed by the longest interludes (for instance section 6) also end with a low, sustained Ab. There is a regular pulse throughout this song, but there does not appear to be a regular patterning of weak and strong beats, each beat seeming as strong as the next. Such a metrical style is sometimes represented with a 1/4 time signature. However, in this transcription no barlines are used, which may allow correspondence between related phrases and passages to be recognized more easily.

Chorus

Cultural background

The vocal music of Ethiopia and neighbouring countries has several characteristics which make it of interest to foreign listeners. Firstly, many of the peoples in this area practise forms of multipart singing which result in a dense and rhythmically intense musical structure. Secondly, much of this vocal music is enlivened by use of a diverse range of sound-producing techniques. These include several forms of yodelling, clapping, the tread of dancing feet and other sounds, such as that of air escaping from a cupped hand suddenly compressed by the performer's armpit.

Some ethnomusicologists argue that the presence of great variety in a musical style means it can be readily appreciated without knowledge of its cultural context. Indeed, one school of thought suggests that the best way for Western listeners to learn to understand musics from around the world is to begin by enjoying the sounds involved. Straightforward aural pleasure, according to this theory, will inspire curiosity about the music's contexts, techniques, instruments and structures. Initial theoretical instruction not only dampens enthusiasm but also implicitly suggests to listeners that such music can only be understood with all its cultural baggage attached.

On the other hand, it has been observed that many prefer listening to music they already know well. New sounds and unfamiliar styles, however colourful, invoke few musical expectations or extra-musical associations for Western listeners, and may thus be quickly rejected. Following this argument, it is necessary to present social and theoretical information as a framework for understanding musical sound.

Teachers might like to test these theories by introducing the two Ethiopian examples in this book in different ways: one with an initial concentration on sound, inspiring subsequent theoretical and contextual discovery, the other with preliminary extra-musical scene-setting developing towards appreciation of the sounds themselves.

Dorzé song

The Dorzé are one of the many peoples inhabiting Ethiopia. Specifically, they are found as farmers and weavers in the mountains in the West of the nation, and also as traders, settlers and migrant workers in other areas. From their contact with the Amhara people, they have adopted a number of musical instruments, such as the *masenqo* fiddle (see Ethiopia: Song with *Masenqo*), but much of their traditional music is vocal. Apart from work songs, love songs and religious music, the Dorzé have the habit of entertaining themselves at festivals and markets through choral song. Texts are improvised to comment on local affairs, or combined from pre-existent fables.

In performance situations, the Dorzé form themselves into several groups, each of which takes a different role. Typically, one group begins the song by repeating a short phrase. After a brief time-lag, the same phrase is taken up by another group, overlapping the first, who continue. A third and fourth group may add the same phrase, once again staggering their entries to overlap with those of the other groups. To this multipart structure are added solo voices; generally each individual takes a short turn of a few lines before returning to the chorus and yielding to another soloist. Finally, clapping or other vocal or physical sounds may be used to give further rhythmic character to the music.

Anthropologists might point to this song structure as a functional model of Dorzé society. A whole social group can perform together, thus affirming communal ties; the performance group is divided into several complementary parts, reflecting the interlocking of different social roles; and there is scope within the group for individual creativity, a metaphor for their balance in society.

Track 2

Dama

The song transcribed was performed as part of the new year celebrations in a Dorzé village. It involves both male and female singers who perform in several parts. Division into parts, however, is not based on the vocal register of the singers. Therefore, there may be both men and women sharing a single part, their voices an octave or a fifth apart. This practice further thickens the texture of the recorded music.

In the segment transcribed, which comes from the middle of a more extended performance, four principal parts can be observed. Shown at the top of the transcription is the solo line. Initially this is sung by a woman, but from bar 10 until the end of the transcription the soloist is a male singer. The text of the solo part mostly repeats the word 'Dama' (also used as the title of this song), generally inserting other syllables in the middle of each bar. The number of syllables, and perhaps the whim of the soloist, affects the choice of melodic and rhythmic patterns for each bar of the solo part, although in basic terms the same pattern can be said to be repeated over and over.

The second stave in the transcription is a group part. This partially overlaps with the solo voice part, covering its rest and providing a sense of antiphony. The third line in the transcription actually conflates at least two, and possibly three, vocable parts. These are difficult to hear at the start of the recording, but can be heard more clearly later on, by which time they have coalesced into an interlocking and reiterated three-note pattern (bar 11). The creation of a composite melodic pattern from pitches produced alternately by different voices (or instruments) is sometimes given the technical name 'hocket'. Some ethnomusicologists now use complicated, multi-track recording techniques in order to aid the separation and transcription of such parts. Finally, the lowest stave shows the regular clapping which continues throughout the whole song.

Song with *Sanza*

Cultural background

The *sanza* is a lamellaphone, or instrument composed of tuned metal rods sounded by the fingers and thumbs. The widespread adoption of this form of instrument across much of Southern, Central and East Africa illustrates the ease with which musical instruments are transmitted from one area to another, and also some of the complications for the music scholar when this occurs. Many different forms of African lamellaphone now exist, together with an equally diverse range of regional names. Noticing a relationship between, say, the *sanza* of the Gbaya people of the Central African Republic and the *mbira* of Shona groups in Zimbabwe is easy enough; explaining when and why this instrumental type was introduced from one area to another is less straightforward.

The Gbaya inhabit western parts of the Central African Republic and eastern areas of Cameroon. Their traditional forms of music-making are predominantly vocal, although some songs are given instrumental accompaniment. One such example is the genre of 'songs of contemplation', a form of music reserved for adult men and performed by them at nocturnal gatherings. While women do not normally take part in the performance of this style, they appear quite commonly as the subjects of song texts, either as named individuals or in general. In both cases, there seems a preference for the women in these songs to be distant and passive objects, appealed to or spoken of by the Gbaya men. Performance style is restrained in terms of volume, and displays of instrumental virtuosity are rare.

The Gbaya, in common with other people in this region, do not have professional musicians, no formal system of musical training exists and no particular prestige attaches to the performance skills of virtuoso players. In some respects, it could be said that the category of 'musician' hardly exists. As such, an informal performance atmosphere prevails, with listeners as free to interject spoken comments or sing choral responses as instrumentalists are free to improvise fresh variations. In some instances, several men perform together and may split the song between them. Also, certain phrases may be performed instrumentally, listeners turning over the words of the song in their minds.

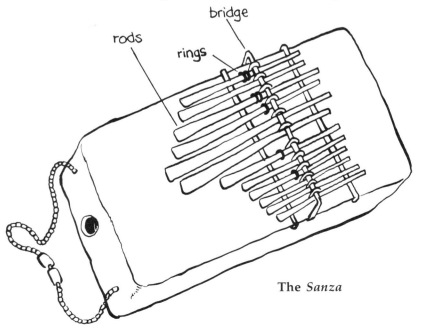

The *Sanza*

Instrumentation

The *sanza* is the primary instrument in the accompaniment of these songs. Typically, it has between eight and twelve metal lamellae, perhaps recast from the spokes of a bicycle wheel or umbrella. The length and thickness of the rod gives each its particular pitch, with a pentatonic scale of approximately two octaves available on larger instruments. These metal rods are passed over a bridge and held in place by a crosswise bar. With one or two exceptions, the longest keys are positioned at the centre of the instrument. Rings are added to some or all of the rods to add sympathetic buzz. The whole is then attached to a wooden box resonator or placed inside a large gourd. In performance, the rods are sounded by the thumbs of both hands, the left thumb playing those to the left of centre and the right thumb those to the right (see previous page).

In some performances of the Gbaya songs of contemplation a pair of lamellaphones are played, in which case the second instrument is sometimes a larger one pitched below the first. Other instruments used in this music are the rattle and the *gàdà* rhythm sticks, which normally maintain a regular pulse throughout.

Songs of contemplation

Musically, these songs consist of a short, reiterated pattern of perhaps eight or twelve beats in duration repeated over and over in varied form. Most performances begin, like this one, with a tentative phrase or two on the *sanza*, gradually establishing the tonality and metrical identity of the song. The players of the rhythm sticks and rattles then join in, giving a regular cycle of two, three or four strokes to each beat, or a composite of these. At the same time, the *sanza* part may become more dense, additional notes being inserted between those initially announced. As the music progresses, the *sanza* may move into different registers, counter-melodies and further decorated forms of the first theme. A second *sanza* may join in, perhaps playing the initial tune or offering a counter-subject of its own. Singing or humming begins, and listeners may feel moved to make responses or to sing group refrains.

 Track 3

Nàá-Ndongoé

The specific example chosen for transcription features two vocalists, both of whom also play *sanza* (the second player can be heard entering at the start of bar 4); there are also rhythm sticks and rattle. The text of this song proposes, and mainly repeats, that when a woman (named Nàá-Ndongoé) is angry she may be pacified through kind words.

After a free-time introductory phrase, the first *sanza* begins to perform the basic pattern which underlies the whole song. The player adds a simple off-beat accompaniment pattern, and emphasizes beats 1 and 5 through repetition of the note given to that beat. The second *sanza* enters in bar 4; during the transcribed excerpt it restricts itself to doubling the main theme of the piece an octave higher. Gradually, the rhythm sticks and rattle are brought in, each with its characteristic rhythmic pattern. The final elements to appear are the two voices, which, after a bar of humming, settle into responsorial mode from bar 11 onwards. Once all parts are established, they continue reworking the same eight-beat pattern.

Although this is a very simple example, much sub-Saharan African music shares the characteristics demonstrated by this song: continuous, varied repetition of a basic musical unit; arrangement of voices in overlapping pairs of call and response; successive entries of new instruments or voices; simultaneous use of contrasting rhythmic patterns; and a preference for enhancing the timbre of melodic instruments with buzzing membranes or vibrating attachments.

Yodelling Exercise

Cultural background   An ethnically diverse nation in West Africa, Gabon is home to, among many other groups, the Baka Bambuké, or Bibayak Pygmies. Traditionally inhabiting equatorial forests in the north of this country, the Baka, like many pygmy groups, hunt and gather food and other necessities in the forest. Since food supply is limited to whatever can be carried back to camp, Baka Bambuké groups have tended to remain fairly small and mobile, a factor which may have encouraged them not to develop heavy and complex musical instruments. Instead, their oldest music is thought to be predominantly vocal, with the whole community normally being involved in a performance. In recent years, additional items, including musical instruments such as the *sanza* lamellaphone (see Central African Republic: Song with *Sanza*), have begun to be bartered or copied from neighbouring tribes, and some musical styles adopted from them also.

Baka Bambuké music   Music is found as part of celebrations, rituals and story-telling, but there also exists a musical game in which women take turns to complete a multipart sequence begun by many voices and drumming, hand-claps or striking sticks together. The idea is to out-sing one another, by demonstrating both vocal power and the ability to sustain a solo pattern against the rhythmic accompaniment. Among this particular group of pygmies, women are considered the better singers, while men tend to dominate the fields of drumming, clapping and dancing, possibly with rattles attached to their ankles to further integrate the dance and music.

Baka Bambuké music has several characteristics of especial note. Firstly, although vocal music predominates, some types of song performance do not have texts. Instead, the Baka Bambuké women alternate a series of open and closed vowel sounds. This combines helpfully with the second notable feature of their music, the women's 'yodelling' technique of singing. The closed vowel sounds (such as 'ee') generally used for higher pitches in this song style require a smaller, less relaxed vocal cavity than the open ones (mainly 'ah' and 'eh') sung deeper in the throat to lower pitches. Thirdly, the melodies in this music most typically consist of chains of alternate rising and falling leaps. Fourth, the traditional tone system uses an equidistant pentatonic scale, i.e. one in which all five notes are evenly spread across the octave. Finally, when multiple singers perform together, they often stagger their entries, and may begin at a different pitch level, factors which have led some to describe this music as 'polyphonic'. Technically, in that the singers may still be singing closely related melodic patterns, albeit at different moments or different pitch levels, it may be more correct to think of this as a form of 'staggered heterophony'. Whatever the technical term, however, the resulting music has a dense and distinctive texture.

 Track 4

Yodelling exercise

Singers need to have a certain confidence in order to be able to contribute their own, seemingly independent parts to a mass performance. To achieve this, the young girls practise with a more experienced, older woman. She sings steadily with them, overseeing their techniques and ensuring that they know when to begin their entries. The transcribed passage is part of just such a rehearsal, one involving two girls led by one woman.

At the start of the excerpt the leader sings alone. Her yodelling pattern consists of three phrases, which last 2, 1½ and 3½ beats respectively. In melodic terms, the three phrases are related, making use of alternate leaps of a fourth or more. On the whole, higher notes are sung to the vowel sound 'ee', while lower ones are prod   ed with 'eh', 'ah' or 'o'. These three phrases are repeated, in sequence, by the leading singer throughout the extract.

The second voice enters at the end of the leader's third phrase. Again, her yodelling pattern is made up of unequally-sized phrases, but in this case there are four phrases, lasting 2½, 1½, 1 and 1 beat in turn. Notably, the second singer's phrases are arranged to rhythmically overlap those of the first voice. The motifs of the second voice contrast with those of the first. The first two include stepwise alternation of C and B♭ before a leap up to F or down to G; the third is a falling pattern, answered by the rising leap of the fourth.

Although the second voice followed on quite quickly after the first, some thirty seconds pass before the third voice enters (bar 9). This part is pitched lower than the other two, ranging from middle C up a seventh to B♭, but again it repeats a six-beat series of melodic patterns which overlap the start and end points of those in the other voices. Once the third singer has established her pattern, the three singers continue the exercise and some occasional melodic variation can be detected.

As mentioned above, this music uses a form of pentatonic scale in which the interval between each pitch is approximately equal, unlike the more commonly encountered 'gapped' pentatonic consisting of major seconds and minor thirds. In the case of this example, this means that the notes transcribed as F and B♭ are actually flatter than Western listeners might expect, while notes transcribed as D are a little sharper. Another way of showing this would be to use an adapted key signature.

Burundi

Whispered Song

Cultural background Burundi is a small but populous nation located in Central Africa. There are three principal ethnic groups, the majority Hutu people, the Tutsi and the Twa pygmies. Until quite recently the Tutsi formed the aristocracy, providing rulers, warriors and cattle-owners; the Hutu were mostly agriculturalists or herders for the Tutsi; and the Twa existed through hunting and engaging in such trades as pottery. Musical performance tends to reflect (and enact) the specific social situations of its creators, and the traditional music of Burundi comprises three distinct repertories, one for each ethnic faction.

The case of Burundi, where distinct musical repertories are associated with differently-employed peoples, sheds useful light on the question of musical 'progress'. Although the idea is now becoming discredited, some still believe that musical style follows a course of development parallel to that of technological progress. Thus, the music of primitive people will be relatively unsophisticated: it will be communal, with perhaps two or three different pitches and few musical instruments. The music of more developed people, on the other hand, will be more complex: it will often involve specialists, with many instruments and a wide range of notes and structures. Put in this way, the theory seems reasonable – societies with larger-scale economies are indeed better able to support professional music-makers, and people with fixed dwellings can accumulate possessions such as heavy or fragile musical instruments beyond the option of nomadic hunters or herders. Analysis of the music of Burundi, however, shows that although the three repertories differ markedly in many key aspects, the music of the Twa hunters is not simpler than that of the Hutu farmers or Tutsi nobility, it is simply different. In certain respects, such as multipart texture and melodic variation, Twa music exhibits greater flexibility than that of the Hutu or Tutsi peoples.

Whispered song

The specific song discussed in more detail below is an example of a musical form now performed by both Hutu and Tutsi men. This is the so-called 'whispered song', a style related to the epic songs once heard at Tutsi courts. Solo song texts typically have a pastoral focus, but within that they embrace a diverse range of subject matter, from historical events (song is often important as a form of record-keeping in non-literate societies) to humorous situations and moral lessons. Praise songs are also a frequently-performed category. Accompaniment is provided by an *inanga* zither, played by the singer, who is generally also the composer of the song and creator of the lyrics. The voice is generally kept low and soft with a breathy timbre which singers believe blends well with the tone of the *inanga*.

The *inanga*

The *inanga* is a form of trough zither. Its body is hollowed from a single piece of wood, up to a metre in length. Notches in both ends allow a single ox tendon to be stretched back and forth across the trough, usually eight times, effectively forming eight strings. These are tuned to a pentatonic scale and plucked with the fingers of both hands. The instrument is held laterally, so that the strings are arrayed vertically and the left hand is above the right.

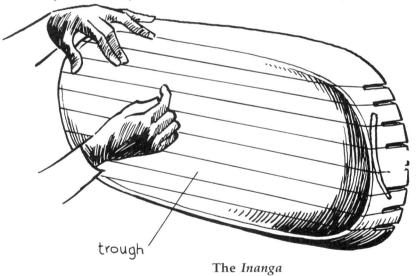

trough

The *Inanga*

Track 5

Praise song

The transcribed passage is apparently part of a song in which the performer praises a benefactor. A translation of the text is not available, so the following analysis concentrates on issues not closely related to language, poetry or text-setting. This is a shame, since many of the Bantu languages of Central Africa are tonal, speech tone contributing toward the meaning of each syllable. Accordingly, it would be interesting to compare the speech contour of the lyrics with the melodic contour of the song. Also, there appears to be a fade-in on the original recording, which suggests that this excerpt may not be the actual beginning of the song in question.

The *inanga* in this recording appears to be tuned to pitches approximately equivalent to B, C♯, D♯, F♯, G♯, A(?), B and c♯. (C♯ and D♯ are a little sharper than those of equal temperament.) B functions as the tonic note, being the accented starting pitch for most segments of the accompaniment. A is very little used, and the music that results is effectively pentatonic.

Initially, the accompaniment consists of a unit of six compound-time beats, repeated or developed over and over to underpin the vocal part. From bar 17 onwards, the basic unit is expanded to a duration of ten beats. Many of the segments used in the accompaniment are closely related, which gives the music greater consistency and permits the singer to concentrate upon the lyrics, but there are also contrasting patterns and varied repeats. These are shown below:

Bar(s)	*Inanga* pattern	Comment (if any)
1	a	simple pattern emphasizing tonic
2–3	b	repeated falling-note pattern; same emphasis; voice starts
4–6	c	alternate rising–falling pattern; tonic emphasis continues
7–9	c'	varied form of pattern c
10–12	c	
13–14	c'	
15–16	d	descending patterns; instrumental interlude
17–24	e	new ten-beat pattern; voice enters at bar 18

The vocal part usually follows the outline of the instrumental melody, and also consists of six- and then ten-beat patterns, which typically begin one beat after those of the accompaniment. The singer uses a hoarse, breathy tone, and some phrases are ended by descending sighs. Text-setting is mostly syllabic, with some phrases and words repeated from one bar to the next. Lines with many syllables have more short-length note values, so that the overall duration of the line is not compromised. Some line-ending syllables rhyme, but the singer does not appear to use a strictly-applied system of rhyming.

Music for *Ingoma*

Cultural background

In many cultures, certain musical instruments are held to symbolize political or religious power. This was the case in historical Burundi too, where the *ingoma* drum ensembles of the principal Tutsi courts represented in musical terms the might and prestige of the rulers. The drums were performed at fixed times of day, at agricultural rites, and accompanied the ruler on travels through his realm. The association between music and power was underlined in performance, with drummers taking turns to sing praises to the ruler. Furthermore, the drums could not be played by just anyone; instead, drummers formed a kind of hereditary clan; although they supported themselves through farming, like other commoners, only they were allowed to play the drums. Recent decades have seen the dissolution of the courts, but the *ingoma* drums have not been abandoned. Rather, the ensemble has been adopted as the primary musical symbol of the nation-state of Burundi.

There is a second area of associations illustrated by the *ingoma* drums, which is the description of their parts with images of fertility. For instance, the body of the drum is referred to as the 'stomach', the skin is described as a 'baby's cradle' and the pegs are likened to a 'mother's breasts'. It would be simple to explain such associations as arising from the use of the ensemble in agricultural rites, but this argument does not explain how the drums first came to be employed in these rituals. Instead, for the traditional inhabitants of Burundi it may have been because of the special power of the drums and their perceived affinity with nature that they were deemed to be effective in agricultural ceremonies.

Use and function

Turning an idea around like this can also be helpful when considering how a particular type of music operates within society. If we employ the term 'use' to

[65]

list the desired effects of a specific music-making event, we can adopt the term 'function' to refer to the actual effects. Often these 'uses' and 'functions' will tend to overlap, but an example shows possible distinctions between the two. Imagine that a man publicly uses a song to tell a woman of his desire to marry her. If she accepts, the song has functioned to aid the creation of a new family unit and the passing of the singer's genes into subsequent generations. Whether successful or not, the song may also have functioned to entertain, infuriate or embarrass various listeners. It has also functioned to provide an opportunity for younger listeners to learn the song themselves.

In the case of *ingoma* drumming from Burundi, we may be correct to observe a similar divergence between use and function. The above-mentioned characteristics of this style – the assertion of political power and the empowerment of agricultural rites – are uses. If, after a performance, the kings and chiefs were accorded greater respect or the crops grew more strongly, these would also be functions. But other functions appear to be present in the performance of this music as well. Notably, these include the display of skill on the part of the drummers and the general enjoyment for audience and drummers alike of an exhilarating musical occasion.

The *ingoma* drum ensemble

A typical ensemble consists of twenty to twenty-five tall, single-headed drums arranged in a semicircle about a central drum. One drummer, holding two wooden sticks, stands at each drum. The performance is begun by the leader, who calls several times to the rest of his team. They cheer in response. Then the drumming begins, with each drummer taking a turn to come forward to the central drum, beating it, dancing and singing praises, again supported by cheers from the whole group. Since the group is large, performances can last a considerable time, but the continuous dancing and gradual variation of the rhythmic patterns maintains audience enjoyment.

 *Track 6*

Ingoma performance

The transcribed passage is the opening of a performance recorded with a single microphone in 1967. Low-pitched drums, which produce low-frequency sounds, are notoriously difficult to record, especially when played as loudly as these, and dance is very much an integral part of the performance, but still this recorded extract gives much of the flavour of the original event.

Apart from the human voice, three principal sounds can be distinguished on the sound-track: beats given a particularly strong emphasis, 'ordinary' beats, and those which sound like the striking of one drum-stick against the other. Sometimes, the first of a group of emphasized beats is preceded by two very fast drum strokes. Through transcribing the patterns of strong beats, the music can be written down in stave notation, although positioning of barlines cannot be seen as authoritative since this may not reflect the units considered significant by the drummers themselves. Still, the transcription reveals that most patterns consist of groups of four or six strikes each. The longer patterns are generally assembled from the shorter ones. For example, bar 14 uses the same pattern as bars 8, 10 and 12, but extends it with an additional six-strike group. The passages in which less rhythmic emphasis occur are those during which a new musician approaches the central drum calling out praise phrases.

Child's Song

Cultural background

Asked to choose a single example of musical sound representative of a particular social group or nation, many would select a piece of music devised and performed by adults, and typically by highly-trained music specialists rather than by ordinary adults. The desire to portray the most special cultural achievements of a society often leads to the presentation of one of its more formal, elaborate types of music-making. Thus, the performance of a professional soloist or royal ensemble is more likely to be chosen as nationally representative than, say, the musical chants of football supporters or the playground songs of school children. This wish to present a positive image of the 'best' is understandable enough, but can lead to the adoption of one or two assumptions about music-making which are worth questioning.

In the first place, we need to keep in mind the fact that examples produced by such a selection procedure may not reflect the most 'typical' or frequently encountered musical situations within a given society. Secondly, if most of the examples selected are of adult musical forms, we may need to remind ourselves that children's music-making is generally rather more than a graded preparation for the styles of adulthood. Not all children's music is taught to them by adults. Instead, many songs and musical games are composed by children or transmitted from one child to another. The musical activities of children can be special and deeply meaningful, equally worthy of investigation as those of older human beings.

To illustrate this point, a Hutu child's song with musical bow accompaniment is included as an example of music from Burundi, alongside a study of this nation's internationally-renowned drum ensemble style (see Burundi: Music for *Ingoma*) and its specialist adult voice with zither style (see Burundi: Whispered Song). This form of singing is performed primarily for self-entertainment, for instance by boys detailed to watch over a herd of cattle or field of crops.

The *umuduri*

In the transcribed song, the singer accompanies himself with a variety of musical bow named the *umuduri*. The basis of this instrument is a curved stick with a metal wire stretched from one end to the other. A hollowed-out gourd is placed a third of the way up the stick, its opening being held against the musician's chest. At this same point, a ring pulls the string close to the gourd resonator. Holding the instrument upright with the left hand, the performer grasps in the right hand two sticks formed into a V-shape. One of these is used to strike the wire string while the other, which may also comprise a seed rattle, is struck against the resonator.

If a seed rattle is used (there is none on the recorded instrument), this adds an extra colour to the sound, and has parallels to the vibrating shells, bottle tops and membranes added to many African musical instruments. Tone quality is also manipulated by the performer, who can move the opening on the gourd resonator closer to or further away from his chest. Closing or partially covering the opening shifts primary resonance from one harmonic of the basic pitch to another. Different fundamental pitches can be achieved by stopping the wire string with the second finger of the left hand.

 *Track 36*

Song with *umuduri*

Although a text is not provided for the transcribed song, songs of this kind typically describe everyday happenings, perhaps mixed with phrases from stories and sayings. As in the example of whispered song, the vocal style is mostly syllabic, and vocal phrases overlap those of the instrumental accompaniment by one beat. Although vocal range is narrow (within an octave), there is still scope for most phrases to demonstrate an overall descending contour to cadence onto G or F (pitched slightly sharper on the recording).

Unlike the whispered song, the transcribed performance maintains a single underlying metrical structure throughout, in this case equivalent to compound quadruple time. This metre is most clearly heard in the *umuduri* part, which reiterates a four-beat pattern as an ostinato to accompany the voice. The first three beats of this ostinato are identical, consisting of a dotted-group rhythm emphasizing the fundamental pitch of the musical bow (C). Only on the fourth beat of the ostinato is this note temporarily departed from, with the performer producing a short scale: E–D–C.

This song is structured similarly to the adult whispered song, however, in that it also uses a handful of patterns repeated over and over, often in developed and extended form. The following diagram charts the re-use of patterns in the transcribed portion of this song. As can be seen, the most usual sequence of phrases is for a two-bar phrase **A** consisting of patterns **a** and **c** to be answered by a related four-bar phrase **A'** made up of patterns **a**, **b**, **c** and **c'**. Sometimes, however, the regularity of this scheme is broken, as for example when bars 14–15 (phrase **A**) are immediately answered by a matching two-bar phrase. Regularity of repetition is also avoided when extra bars are inserted in the middle of a phrase, for instance bar 8 which converts that repetition of phrase **A** into a three-bar unit, or bars 22, 23 and 25 which extend their respective version of phrase **A'** to seven bars in length.

	Phrase A			Phrase A'						
Pattern	a	b	c	a	b	d	b	c	c	c'
Bar:	1	–	2	3	4	–	–	5	–	6
	7	8	9	10	11	–	–	12	–	13
	14	–	15							
	16	–	17							
	18	–	19	20	21	22	23	24	25	26

Mozambique

Music for *Timbila*

Cultural background

The xylophone-based orchestral music of the Chopi people of Mozambique has acquired an international reputation as a particularly complex musical tradition. The Chopi inhabit coastal areas towards the southern end of Mozambique, fairly close to South Africa, where many Chopi men have worked as migrant mine workers. Some scholars believe this coastal location is significant, suggesting that the use of large xylophone ensembles in this area is the result of past cultural contact between this part of Africa and Indonesia.

During colonial times, each Chopi chief maintained his own *timbila* ensemble, its size and quality being representative of his status. Singers advanced their chief's viewpoint in their lyrics, and the discipline and strength of an ensemble was further emphasized by the co-ordinated movements of a team of dancers. Political rivalries were often expressed through musical performance, with rival ensembles performing simultaneously, each one trying to out-do the others and thereby win greater support for its sponsor. More recently, *timbila* ensembles were founded at South African mines, where they served an entertainment function for the workers, as well as an outlet for their political aspirations. Finally, since independence from Portugal (1975), orchestras have been organized as weekend activities by local government officials. In each of these cases, the relationship between music-making and power is of great significance, and music functions as a non-violent means of political argument.

Timbila

Timbila (singular *mbila*) is the collective term among the Chopi for xylophones and their music. Several different-sized xylophones are found in a Chopi orchestra, but all are constructed of a series of finely-tuned wooden keys tied onto a rectangular wooden frame. Beneath each key is a hollow gourd resonator, again carefully tuned, and finished with a membrane-covered opening. This feature adds a distinctive buzz to the sound of the instruments. In performance, the keys are struck with hammers held in both hands, experienced players sustaining independent rhythmic or melodic patterns in each. These techniques take much practice to acquire, and successful Chopi musicians must devote considerable time from childhood onwards to developing their mastery.

The largest *mbila* has only four keys and provides a rhythmic drone. Ranged above it to occupy a composite musical spectrum of four octaves are four higher-pitched instruments with overlapping registers. The higher xylophones usually have between twelve and nineteen keys, which are tuned to an equidistant heptatonic scale. (Each step in this seven-note scale is a little smaller than a Western whole tone but none is as small as a semitone). Multiple xylophones of each type are used, with a respectable orchestra likely to number at least twelve xylophonists. There are also rattles, generally performed by the dancers, which add a regular rhythmic pulse to the music. In some dances whistles and drums may be added as well.

The most traditional music for this instrumental ensemble consists of suites lasting approximately an hour, comprising perhaps ten instrumental movements, dances and songs. Within each piece, a tune or sequence of tunes is repeated or varied over and over. Characteristics of this repertory include many forms of rhythmic development, very often involving two-against-three patterns, and chordal accompaniment based largely on fourths, fifths and octaves. Passages in strict unison contrast with longer sections where performers deliberately thicken the texture through individual heterophony. An orchestral leader, often the composer of the suite, directs each performance through a series of visual and aural cues which must be memorized and obeyed by the other musicians.

Owing to its complexity, there are major problems in accurately transcribing such music. Ethnomusicologists have used two main methods of overcoming these. One is to learn how to play the music themselves, which normally means living for an extended time among the people in question and learning to play much as an apprentice musician there would. Armed with this practical experience, the scholar can then usually write down the music. Alternatively, the ethnomusicologist may begin by recording the whole band together, then play back the track through headphones to each performer in turn. Whilst listening to the performance, the musician plays his own part again, which is picked up by a second tape recorder. Each part can then be taken down individually and a complete score gradually built up. Unfortunately, neither method was practicable in this case, and the resulting transcription must be seen as a very partial reflection of Chopi musical characteristics.

 Track 8

Mabandla

The 'Dance of the Councillors' demonstrates many of the key features of Chopi xylophone music, including its fast tempo, rattle accompaniment, virtuosic performance skills, cross-rhythmic patterning, dense texture alleviated by periodic unison phrases, cyclic form and occasional use of descending, syllabic vocal melodies. The passage transcribed shows the conclusion of the dance.

A fast, eight-beat pattern is the basis of this dance. The beat is subdivided by the rattles, which keep up a regular pulsation until the very end of the dance. The tonic pitch is approximately B, and most of the *timbila* return either to this note or to F♯ at the beginning of each eight-beat cycle. The vocal entries consist of pairs of descending phrases. Four of these are shown on the transcription, the first (bars 9–12) being for solo voice, and the other three for two-part male chorus. One section of the chorus sings a figure based on the soloist's descending tune, to which the other section responds with an answering phrase. Various other sounds are woven into the composition, including whistles, claps and shouts.

Play Song

Cultural background
Russian folk music has great regional variety, as might be expected in a nation of such size and ethnic diversity. Modernization, urbanization and political change have led to the abrupt discontinuation or dramatic adaptation of many musical traditions in Russia, but in some communities older styles of music-making have been retained. This discussion concentrates on these areas (though the adaptation of traditional musics for use in the modern world is also worthy of study). It also concentrates on vocal forms, although there are many fascinating types of Russian instrumental music, from panpipe ensembles to solo accordion music, as well as important musical styles which use both instruments and voices.

Amongst the traditional vocal repertories of the many different Russian regions, many songs can be categorized as 'calendrical'. These are songs related to religious and agricultural events, such as New Year, sowing or harvest-time. Some contain important lore reminding the singers how they should carry out a particular activity or ritual. The primary function of others is to create a mood appropriate to the event itself. Members of Russian rural communities also perform work songs, although this is a repertory upon which agricultural, domestic and industrial mechanization has had a major impact. There are many songs marking and celebrating the different stages of the wedding ritual, and also lullabies, songs for childbirth, children's game-songs, and laments sung at funerals both by relatives of the deceased and by hired professional mourners. Apart from these, other songs allow scope for the expression of individual feelings and for the telling of stories.

In Russia, as in many other societies, it has been observed that older women play an important role in maintaining and transmitting traditional musical heritage. Often, they do so not as professional teachers or performers, roles which men would more typically have assumed in the past, but as more informal ensembles. Nonetheless, they may be highly valued by their villages, and asked to perform publicly upon important occasions.

 Track 9

Play Song

The transcribed song is used for entertainment purposes. It is sung by a group of women while younger girls dance, and comes from the village of Kieba in Siberia. This particular song illustrates some of the vocal textures found in Russian folk song, which range from simple monodic phrases to more broadly developed multipart pieces. Many Russian songs use call and response form, contrasting a solo opening phrase with a group reply. This is reflected in this song, although only the first verse follows this pattern. Like certain other Russian songs, each verse sets a short line of text, most phrases here having eight or nine syllables, often including one or more repeated words. These words are supplemented by padding syllables.

The song is performed without instrumental accompaniment and within a fairly narrow vocal range (approximately an octave). B is the fundamental of the song, providing the starting and ending notes, while E is of secondary importance. The choral part of the song alternates between passages of unison and passages of thirds. However, one aspect not shown in the transcription is that each singer within the group is free to perform either the melody note or an accompanying pitch a third below, and can alternate between these as the chorus progresses. In metrical terms, the song falls mostly into simple duple time, but the final bar of each verse and chorus is extended by a beat. Decorative elements such as pitch slides are also characteristic of this singing-style.

The song has two basic phrases, one in the upper part of the register and one which zigzags across the whole octave. The first phrase is four bars in length and the second five (including the extra beat). In verse 1 phrase **A** is given to a solo singer, but from the first entry of phrase **B** the whole song is sung by a group of female voices. This performance of the song has a total of six verses.

Summary-translation

> Oh, meadow berry,
> Oh young girl!
> Where have you been walking?
> I was walking through the open country,
> I was sitting under the bush,
> Under the raspberry's leaf.

In that this is a humorous song, we may be correct to guess that the young girl was not spending her time alone 'under the bush'.

Hymn

Cultural background

Armenia is located in the Caucasus between Turkey and Russia. Perhaps because their nation has regularly been dominated by a succession of neighbouring larger powers, Armenians have striven to maintain a distinctive culture, and features of their music can be traced back many centuries. This music includes modal Christian chant (Armenia was the first nation to convert to Christianity, in 301 A.D.), several styles of professional and amateur folk singing, and a wealth of instrumental music, much of which reflects the influence of Middle Eastern and Central Asian styles.

Apart from rural song traditions specific to each locality, there are also urban folk song and ensemble traditions. Classes of professional entertainers are also documented, ranging from the recounters of epics to dancers and poets. Amongst them, beginning during the late eighteenth century, were various schools of *ashughner*, itinerant musicians who developed virtuoso skills at improvisation. These musicians also composed, creating their own poetry and melodies, and accompanying themselves during performance on an instrument such as the *saz* or *tar* long-necked lutes, *k'anon* zither, *sant'ur* dulcimer or *k'amancha* spike fiddle. Traditional Armenian music demonstrates both polyphonic and antiphonal textures, solo and unison singing, and the employment of a drone bass accompaniment.

Religious music in Armenia

The song recorded and transcribed is an example of Armenian liturgical chant. Chant is central to the Armenian Church. Documentation of the oldest chants dates from approximately five hundred years ago, but oral tradition and some earlier manuscripts lead Armenian historians to ascribe certain chants to the fourth century. Little is known of the music of this period. However, during the eighth century it is known that Armenian clerics adopted a system of eight modes, one for each week of an eight-week cycle. This system is thought to have originated in or near Jerusalem in the early seventh century, and was subsequently adopted in Western Europe by the singers of the Gregorian chant tradition. Modes were not simply sets of notes within which hymn-singing took place but also models for performance. Today, however, more than eight modes are found, so reconstructing the early Armenian Church music is difficult.

One factor that could help in this task is the existence of musical notation in Armenian hymn manuscripts from the ninth century onwards. In this notation, melodic rises and falls, standard melodic or rhythmic patterns and expression marks are shown above each word in the hymn text. Unfortunately, certain features of this means of notation are not clear today, since during some periods oral transmission was relied upon to pass on the music. Today, a much simplified form is used, as well as staff notation.

Hymns are now performed by secular male-voice choirs as well as by monks. Either of two performance textures is usual: solo or unison (monophony), or unison melody over a drone bass. No instrumental accompaniment is used. In some hymns the bass drone note may shift, perhaps down a step, although it generally returns to the opening pitch before the hymn ends.

Track 10

Ognagan Induneli Egher

The transcribed hymn, 'Accept my prayer, oh God', is a resurrection chant attributed to Step'annos Siunetsi (eighth century). Siunetsi is believed to have established the eight-mode system in Armenia and composed several hymns. This hymn has two sections, each based on the drone note A. In the first section, a mode equivalent to the Western harmonic minor scale (starting on A) is used. In the second, the mode is equivalent to the diatonic major scale (again starting on A), although in two phrases there is use of B♯, a note which leads towards the secondary tonal centre C♯. The secondary tonal centre of the first section is F, the note upon which two of its phrases end. Apart from the difference of mode, the melody line in the second section is pitched in a higher register: section 1 moves between e and c', section 2 between a and f♯'. Section 2 is also a little faster than the first section.

Nonetheless, the two sections fit well together. Apart from their common drone note, there is symmetry between their alternate emphasis of A and the note a third below (section 1) or above (section 2). Also, although they do not share melodic material, both sections have a similar blend of unmetred, smooth, melismatic quavers and stepwise, syllabic crotchets. Another connection can be found in the manner in which the melody in each section is built out of short, adaptable motifs:

Distributional Analysis of *Ognagan Induneli Egher*, **Section 1**

Note: in this style of analysis, phrases are stretched to align common material vertically.

Music for *K'amancha*

Cultural background

Although Armenian chant (see Armenia: Hymn) has certain similarities with Russian and other forms of Christian religious music, Armenian instrumental styles have strong parallels among Middle Eastern and Central Asian musical traditions, especially those of Iran. Within the same instrumental type, the music performed by rural amateurs can be quite distinct from that of professional entertainers. Armenian music for the *k'amancha* spike fiddle forms a case in point, where the number of strings and pattern of tuning varied from folk to professional performers' instruments.

As a folk instrument, the *k'amancha* was performed as a solo and mixed ensemble instrument for entertainment, for instance at weddings. In urban areas, the *k'amancha* was also known as an instrument played by the professional *ashughner* itinerant musicians who were as adept at musical performance as they were at improvisation, composition and poetics. During the twentieth century a new category of instrumentalist arose, state-supported and possibly conservatory-trained, who performed in public concerts and on radio broadcasts. In the 1930s, some of these musicians formed a quintet of different-sized *k'amancha*, performing together as an ensemble. Innovations of this kind can feed back to the countryside, where rural musicians attempt to imitate in their own performance contexts the styles they hear broadcast on national radio. However, the example transcribed is more traditional, being the performance of a single *k'amancha*.

[73]

The *k'amancha*

Although some traditional instruments have three strings, the contemporary art music *k'amancha* normally has four metal strings, tuned to a, e', a' and e" (or like the violin with the lowest two strings raised a tone). In structure, the *k'amancha* is somewhat like the Ethiopian *masenqo* (see Ethiopia: Song with *Masenqo*), being a spherical body faced with skin or membrane transfixed by a long wooden shaft. The lower part of this shaft is attached to a spike which protrudes below the instrument's body to balance on the player's left knee. The upper part acts as a fingerboard and, at the very top, a receptacle for the tuning pegs. As with some other spike fiddles, for example the Greek *lyra* (see Greece: 1930s Folk Dance), the instrument is partially rotated during performance to bring one of its strings into contact with the bowhair. The bowhair, as on instruments such as the European viol or Chinese *erhu*, is pressed by the fingers to tighten it whilst playing.

Track 11

Life is but a Window

This short composition exemplifies the improvisatory style of some solo Armenian *k'amancha* pieces. It is performed in a free rhythmic manner, with brief pauses between each phrase, and the metre is not fixed. This does not mean that the performer's interpretation of each phrase is random or arbitrary; that relative note durations are carefully calculated by the *k'amancha*-player is demonstrated by the fact that on the repeat, the phrases are played very closely the same. Indeed, the most immediately apparent difference between the first rendition and the second is that the final two phrases are played twice the second time.

This piece also offers an example of how scales in Armenian art music are structured in a way somewhat akin to those in Iran (see Iran: Art Music for Ensemble). The pitches chosen for a piece of music come from various interlocking segments of three or four pitches each, not from scales or modes conceived as distinct, seven-note entities.

The note which functions as the fundamental of this piece is E, with G being of secondary importance. All phrases other than the first cadence to one or other of these two pitches. Within the composition, movement is mostly by step rather than by leap, another feature also found in Middle Eastern art music, and the *k'amancha* remains in a narrow segment of its register. Some phrases are interrelated, for instance the music of phrase 4 returns as phrase 9. Overall, the composition is structured as below:

Phrase	Comments
1	Opening flourish introducing the upper segment of the register (C and high D)
2	Highly ornamented passage linking this segment to that below it (C, B♭, A and G). Basically, this phrase is a decorated fall to the secondary cadential note G.
3	Similar to phrase 2, this one repeats the descending pattern and continues it to present the third and lowest segment used in this piece (G, F, E and low D).
4	Phrase 4 reiterates and develops a G–F–E falling pattern, underlining the importance of E as the fundamental.
5 & 6	Variety is introduced through use of contrasting mid-range and mid- to low-register segments, again cadencing to G and E.
7	After this brief excursion, there is a return to the original mode, presented from high to low in a style reminiscent of phrase 2 and 3.
8	Development of the mid and low segments in an arch-shape phrase.
9	The pattern from phrase 4 returns to round off the verse.

The whole verse is then repeated, with minor differences, and the final two phrases performed one extra time to complete the composition, all of which is found on the accompanying recording.

Work Song 1

Cultural background

Georgia is a small, multi-ethnic nation located in the area between Russia, Turkey and the Middle East. As such, its musical life has been subject to a number of strong but contrasting influences. For example, the Georgian Church established its own rites, which included sacred music, as early as the fourth century. During periods when some or all of Georgia was ruled by Islamic peoples, primarily the years from 1555 to the nineteenth century when it was divided between Persia and Turkey, Middle Eastern musical forms were adopted, at least amongst the upper classes. There was also Russian-influenced art music, including operas, symphonies and chamber music, which were performed in Georgia from the 1820s onward. Coupled with these was a Nationalist movement, when numerous folk songs were collected and published, often in arrangements for chorus or European musical instruments.

Georgian folk music

As well as the various art musics mentioned above, each region of Georgia is characterized by different styles of folk song, with particularly marked differences between styles preferred in the East and the West of the country. In general, Georgian folk song is often described as 'polyphonic', a term which suggests that several parts simultaneously perform rhythmically-independent melodic lines. Many Georgian folk songs do indeed have one, two or three solo male voices performing melodically above a slower-moving group bass. The simplest songs set a single melody above a drone bass. Others alternate the melody between two soloists. In the most complex songs, the upper voices move homophonically above a drone or ostinato bass. Strictly speaking, none of these examples is polyphony as defined above, but the high value placed on polyphony in European art music has led folk music scholars and musicians to apply these terms to their music as well.

Multipart songs are most widespread among the peoples of Western Georgia. Apart from choruses, there are also solo men's work songs, women's lullabies, and narrative songs. All of these may also have instrumental accompaniment. Solo songs are found primarily in Eastern Georgia, although singing in two or three parts is also common there.

Kartalin work songs

The Kartalin people are classified among the Eastern Georgians. Their solo, unaccompanied work songs typically involve the setting of the same free-rhythm melody to several stanzas of text. Each stanza begins in high register and falls, with periods of syllabic, recitative-like music contrasting with those of more melismatic ornamentation. The singer selects a traditional melodic formula to act as the backbone of the specific song, and is guided by the text of each line as he improvises rhythmic and melodic perambulations.

Track 12

Ourmouli

The transcribed song, 'The Wagoner', is associated with a traditional ox-drawn cart, or *ouremi*. Unfortunately, details of its words are not known. There are six stanzas, each of which has three elements, all in free metre. The first is recitative-like in style, consisting of a series of syllables on a repeated note, a rising melody or a combination of the two (stanza 1 is an exception). The second element is in its simplest form (stanza 2) a descending scale from a sustained high note, all sung to the same syllable. In more complex stanzas (for instance, phrase 4) the melody may fall, slowly rise and fall again. The final element usually consists of a sustained pitch decorated through alternation with the note a step higher, and then a fall down to the cadential note, which is also sustained in most stanzas. Unlike the syllabic style of the first element, the third is more melismatic, allowing greater scope for musical invention.

Melodically, this song demonstrates the improvisatory treatment of the overall falling melodic contour typical of Kartalin work songs. Thus, the first element begins in, or rises to, the upper part of the register. The second moves even higher but begins the descent. The third seems to suspend the descent, with its opening sustained note and upwards alternation, but then it too moves down, such that all phrases are completed on the lowest pitch of the song, Bb. The example below compares a phrase of the song with a melodic outline showing the main pitches used in each phrase.

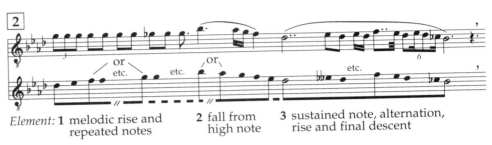

Element: **1** melodic rise and repeated notes   **2** fall from high note   **3** sustained note, alternation, rise and final descent

Phrase 2 and Melodic Skeleton of *Ourmouli*

Modally, it is difficult to describe *Ourmouli* precisely. Most phrases end on Bb, and other important notes are Db and F; both G and Gb are used, which suggests a mode equivalent to the diatonic minor scale. However, Cb is as common as C, and E♮ is often found. If the basic scale is taken as Bb, Cb, Db, Eb, F, Gb, Ab this song could be described as using the phrygian mode; if, on the other hand, C is preferred to Cb, aeolian mode would be appropriate; and, finally, if C and G are preferred to Cb and Gb, dorian mode offers a reasonable description of the song. Perhaps it is better to say that it uses a heptatonic scale based on Bb with flexible second, fourth and sixth degrees.

Work Song 2

Cultural background

This unit, like the previous one, concentrates on a Georgian work song. Elsewhere in this book, when multiple examples from the same music culture are presented they are from different genres (for instance a work song followed by an instrumental piece or hymn). In this case, the point of selecting two examples from the same musical category and area is that while it is useful to study different genres it is also necessary to understand the possible range of variety within the same traditional genre. Unless there are powerful social reasons discouraging innovation – as in some forms of religious and magical performance – human music-making tends to be a diverse and creative activity.

Two Kartalin work songs

The work song studied previously was of the solo kind. That discussed here is a two-part song for soloist and (unison) chorus of eight men. The previous example was free-metre and incorporated both syllabic and melismatic elements; the bulk of this song is strictly metrical (compound quadruple time) and almost exclusively syllabic. The first song consisted of six stanzas, each comprising several freely-interpreted melodic and rhythmic elements; the second song has two distinct sections, one repeating an alternating series of short solo 'calls' and simple choral ostinato, the other a through-composed passage based primarily on pitched shouts tossed back and forth between the soloist and one member of the chorus.

Nonetheless, this song is not entirely unlike the earlier one. As in the previous example, the leader in this one is able to extemporize new phrases of text as the song continues. There is no need for these phrases to have any relation to the work in hand; indeed, if the task is a dull or arduous one, then the principal function of the song would be to entertain the singers, distracting them from the drudgery of their work. Further similarities include the high vocal range of the leading voice and the frequent employment of pitch slides.

 *Track 13*

Herio da Hopouna

The 'Song of the Sifters', as already mentioned, has two sections. The first is opened by a call phrase from the soloist. The chorus respond with their three-note ostinato pattern, always sung to the vocables, 'A-hey-hey'. Upon their entry, it appears that some of the chorus have mispitched their first note, it taking another note for them to find the same pitch. The third note of the ostinato overlaps with the second entry of the soloist, who re-uses a falling pattern (F♯–E–D–B) from bar 1. The soloist's final note, which is more called-out than sung, overlaps with the next choral entry. The song continues in this way for some time, the soloist using three different melodic patterns: that already described, a similar one in which a high G♯ replaces the initial F♯ and a contrasting, lower-pitched phrase moving from B to D and back. All the while, interest is maintained by a gradual acceleration.

The second section of this song is quite different. It begins with the soloist performing a kind of simultaneous trill and descending slide, immediately echoed by the chorus. Thereafter, a pair of called-out phrases are heard and, following a sustained cry from the soloist, he and another singer exchange repeated cries a semitone apart. This happens four times, with five, three, two and three cries respectively.

Judging from the solo part in section 1, the solo singer uses a hexatonic scale: B, C♯, D, E, F♯ and G♯, although G♯ occurs more as a substitute for F♯ than as its neighbour. The chorus sing just two pitches, A (not used by the soloist) and B, a pattern which reinforces the feel of B as the fundamental of this particular song.

Professional Folk Music

Cultural background

The folk music tradition of Romania includes songs closely linked to the main events of the life-cycle: birth, marriage and death. Other than these, there are also songs designed primarily for entertainment, and instrumental music, much of which is intended for dancing. Entertainment songs fall into three principal categories: the strophic song, the *doina* and the ballad. In the strophic song the same music serves as the basis for a series of different verses. In the past, regional styles were quite distinct. The *doina*, however, was stylistically more unified across Romania, and relied upon an improvisatory melody which followed the mood of the singer. The ballad is described in more detail below. Instrumental music uses some of these structures and styles also, and it is common for songs and dances to be combined.

Instrumentation

Until recently, in the region of Wallachia, much music-making was put in the hands of professional gypsy musicians. These musicians were adept at several instruments as well as singing, and typically arranged themselves into a *taraf*, possibly a family-based band. Such an ensemble had a variable instrumentation but often included a *vioara* violin (the leading instrument), *nai* panpipes and *cobză* lute (similar in appearance to the Middle Eastern *'ūd*). More recently, a *tambal* dulcimer, accordion and *contrabas* double bass have become standard accompanying instruments to the violin, with the lute and panpipes disappearing.

In the recorded example, the leader of the *taraf* performs the *vioara* as well as singing the story. When singing, he sometimes doubles his vocal melody with the violin. He is accompanied by *tambal* and *contrabas*, the latter played more as a rhythmic ostinato accompaniment than a harmonic bass-line. In the main, the *tambal* player fills in harmonies to accompany the melody, but may take short melodic phrases between lines of the verse.

The ballad

In Wallachia, the ballad is referred to as a 'song of old', or *cîntec bătrînesc*. In these ballads several verses freely vary a flexible melody on each repetition. Before each verse there is often a *taxîm*, or improvisatory instrumental prelude based on the melody of the song. As the word *taxîm* suggests, there has been a considerable Middle Eastern influence on Romanian musical traditions. Ballad texts may be romantic, heroic, humorous or fantastic, and may tell a story or illustrate a moral point. The ballad is generally found as part of a suite, perhaps being coupled with other songs or followed by a series of dances. In the performance recorded there were originally eleven verses, each preceded by an instrumental *taxîm*. These lead into two circle-dances and a further fast, syncopated dance.

 *Track 14*

Sarpele

The excerpt recorded and transcribed comes from a ballad known as 'The Serpent', a legendary tale telling how a widow bore a son whilst a serpent lurked around the home. The widow sees the presence of the snake as an evil omen and foretells that her son will be killed by such a serpent. Although the serpent is eventually slain, the boy's fate remains unchanged: he is subsequently killed by a different serpent.

The transcription shows the first *taxîm* and verse 1. The *taxîm* begins with the leader playing a phrase which falls, much decorated, from high G to B♭ (bar

1). This pattern is then repeated (bar 2). A second musical idea is introduced in bar 3. This phrase contrasts rhythmically, modally (Db instead of Dᵇ) and in melodic contour although it also falls to end on Bb. In bar 4 the second idea is repeated. This time, its latter segment (the fall to Bb) is extended to lead down to G (bar 5), a process which is then repeated. A simple link (bar 7) returns to Bb before the start of verse 1. Verse 1 also has pairs of repeated phrases. The phrase structure for the first part of the verse is as follows:

Bars	Phrase	Comments
8–12	A	stepwise descent from F, through Eb and D, to Bb
13–14	link	
14–18	A'	varied repeat of A beginning on Eb
18–21	B	stepwise rise from Bb to Db and back again
22–25	B	repeat of B
25–27	C	extension of B melody down to low G
28–32	C'	varied repeat of C

This structure is then repeated in the second part of the verse. Thus, both the *taxîm* and the verse are built from the same basic melodic structure of three repeated phrases gradually working down a heptatonic scale to low G. Nonetheless, there is considerable rhythmic contrast between the free-metre *taxîm* and the more regular verse. The verse itself sets units of two against units of three, the melody alternating between compound duple and simple triple time, whilst the rhythmic pulse of the *contrabas* suggests simple duple metre.

The mode used is: G, A (or Ab), Bb, C, D (or Db), Eb (or E) and F, with phrases typically cadencing to Bb and G. The *contrabas* generally reiterates Bb or G, decorating it with the pitch a fourth lower. Both D and Db are used in the melody and its accompaniment, although Db is perhaps a little more common. Both A and Ab are found in the tune, generally Aᵇ in lower octaves but Ab in higher ornamental passages. These notes (D and A) are considered 'neutral' – they may be performed either as natural, flat, or midway between natural and flat. Eb is more usual than E in the melody. When Eᵇ does appear it is most often part of a scale from Dᵇ up to F.

Music for *Cimpoi*

Cultural background

The *doina*, unlike many of Romania's communal and life-cycle-related musical traditions, is a more directly personal means of expression in which a single performer adapts an improvisatory melody to follow his or her mood. *Doine* (plural) are both sung and performed instrumentally. Texts are often poems of grief, regret or social injustice, although in some regions a love *doina* with erotic words is found. That recorded is an example of the former type, a Moravian *doina di jele*, or mourning *doina*.

This performance is given on the *cimpoi* bagpipe, an instrument not played by professional *taraf* musicians (see Romania: Professional Folk Music) but by shepherds and peasants. It is derived from a historical recording collected in the first half of the twentieth century, before political change, increasing agricultural mechanization and the spread of radio and cassette technology began to transform the working and listening habits of Romania's rural population.

The *cimpoi*

Known since the fifteenth century, six different types of *cimpoi* are found across Romania. That recorded has a windbag of sheepskin or goatskin and the external appearance of having two pipes and a blow pipe. In reality the bagpipe has three sounding pipes, the melodic chanter and a middle drone pipe being encased in a single tube (see overleaf). The middle pipe can be extended by use of a detachable length of tube. In the middle pipe there is a single hole, which allows the player to alternate between notes a fourth apart. In the chanter there are six finger-holes and one thumb-hole, which are fine-tuned by being partially covered with wax.

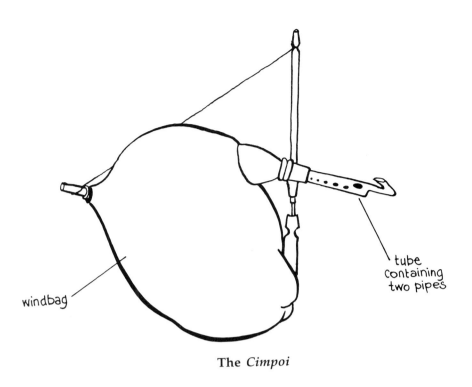

The *Cimpoi*

windbag

tube
containing
two pipes

Track 15

Doina di jele

Structurally, *doine* are usually quite freely formed and free in metre – especially instrumental *doine*, where the musician is not restricted by the need to pronounce a text clearly. As in certain other improvisatory styles, performances are assembled by adding phrases or parts of phrases freely one after another, rather than by elaborating upon a preconceived structural outline.

Most phrases of the transcribed *doina* are fairly short and end on the fundamental pitch C. At the beginning of the performance, the musician mainly plays decorated falling phrases. Subsequently, more elaborate patterns of rising and falling notes are introduced. To link phrases on the chanter pipe, and at other times as well, there is often an alternation of C and G on the middle pipe, which helps to maintain rhythmic momentum whilst the player decides what to do melodically in the next phrase. Several times during the performance, however, this does not occur; at these places, the piper simply maintains a C drone on all three pipes. (The transcription halts at the second of these).

As mentioned, the fundamental of the piece is C, sustained on the lower pipe. C is alternated with G on the middle pipe. The chanter ranges predominantly between C and G, mainly employing the notes C, D, E♭, F♯ and G, although a pair of grace notes (high A and low B) lie outside this range. Counting just the main notes, the scale which results might be described as pentatonic, although it is not the same as the more familiar 'gapped' pentatonic which ranges over a whole octave (for example, C, D, E, G, A, C). A better description might be that the melody typically remains within a fifth section of a heptatonic scale consisting of C, D, E♭, F♯, G, A and B. This restricted melodic range results from the limited range of notes available on the chanter pipe.

Nonetheless, despite its narrow melodic range the piece has a rich, three-strand texture, one line emanating from each pipe. This texture can be described as melody with drone accompaniment, the bass drone being doubled either two octaves or an octave and a fifth higher.

Greece

Village Wedding Music

Cultural background

Greek folk music exists in several distinct regional traditions, and includes instrumental as well as vocal genres. Many of these have been influenced by neighbouring foreign styles; Greece was itself part of the Ottoman Turkish Empire for an extended period, perhaps accounting for the many elements of Turkish musical style still found in Greece. Whatever its region of origin, traditional music is performed in many of the same contexts in insular and continental Greece, particularly at weddings, funerals and other communal occasions. Other kinds of urban entertainment music have also developed, both in Greece and amongst Greek communities overseas, and offer fascinating examples of musical cross-fertilisation.

The example studied here illustrates this same idea, although a little less dramatically. Throughout the last century, certain older Greek folk instruments have gradually been abandoned in favour of newer or foreign-derived alternatives. For instance, the *gaida* bagpipe has since the nineteenth century largely given way to the *klarino* clarinet. The *klarino* is heard leading the ensemble on this recording, which was made at a village wedding in the late 1960s. This instrument is accompanied by an ensemble of violin, lute, tambourine and drum. (The violin is indistinct on the recording and has been omitted from the transcription. Usually, we would expect the violinist to double the clarinet melody in heterophonic style.) The musicians are playing outside a small church, entertaining those unable to squeeze inside to watch the service itself. This particular performance, then, is not part of the formal wedding ritual itself.

Although the clarinettist exploits the wide range and chromatic potential of his instrument, its part retains two characteristics suggestive of the *gaida*. First, a constant melodic line is maintained almost throughout the entire performance, broken only by occasional breathing spaces. Second, the clarinettist plays mostly in a legato style, articulating the melody through the inclusion of numerous, fast finger-ornamentations.

 *Track 16*

Kalamatianos

The *kalamatianos* is a fast dance in 7/8 metre, and is now popular over much of Greece. Each bar of the 7/8 metre is subdivided into units of 3+2+2. Some Western classical musicians would call this an 'irregular' metre, referring to the differing lengths of the beats. However, we should remember that this metrical subdivision is employed quite consistently throughout the dance; to the musicians and their accustomed listeners, this metre probably seems perfectly 'regular'. Regularity is also exhibited by the phrase structure of the *kalamatianos*, which relies mainly on two- and four-bar units. Variety is ensured through the performers' creative decoration of the tune and rhythm as the dance progresses. Even immediate repeats of short motifs are often slightly varied. An overall ternary shape may be proposed, from the point of view of tonality, with the opening and closing passages using a scale equivalent to B♭ major and the central portion passing through other modes.

Typically in this dance form, the listeners arrange themselves in a circle to dance. A leader may occupy the centre of the circle and perform acrobatics. Some other dance forms offer the leading musician the chance to perform an unmetred improvisation, a kind of musical parallel to the chief dancer's acrobatics. In this specific case, recorded in Epirus, the ensemble launch straight into the dance itself, with a few chords from the lute providing a lead-in. At the end of the dance, the clarinet provides a similarly brief cadential pattern.

1930s Folk Dance

The music introduced below is an example of an archive recording from a museum. In 1929, the young man Samuel Baud-Bovy visited Greece in order to research its folk musical traditions. At that time, many European music scholars were concerned that changes in living style were leading to the disappearance of valuable folk traditions which they felt had existed, perhaps unchanged, for a very long time. They therefore attempted to collect and preserve as much of this musical heritage as they could, using wax cylinders, 78 r.p.m. records or whatever technology they could acquire. They hoped that their interest in folk music would encourage its performers to keep to the traditional ways of doing things, and some of these scholars (but not Baud-Bovy) tried to prevent the spread of newer styles by only recording the oldest, most conservative repertory and by criticizing or ignoring more innovative musicians. The recordings were then kept safely in archives where they could be studied, and perhaps transcribed into music notation for publication.

Most ethnomusicologists now believe that folk musical traditions tend towards constant change, unless there is strong social pressure to keep innovation at a minimum, as for example in ritual styles where unusual sounds might distract the listeners or spoil the power or sanctity of the rite. Because change is a usual state of affairs, it may not be either possible or desirable to preserve a musical style, and newly-created and adapted folk traditions are now as widely studied as older ones. Nonetheless, the extensive collections of recordings so painstakingly gathered by people such as Baud-Bovy, and the studies they based upon them, remain of great value, in that we can assess musical change by comparing them with more recent recordings.

The recording analysed below is performed by two musicians from the island of Karpathos, located midway between the isle of Crete and the Turkish mainland. Baud-Bovy invited these musicians, one of whom was a personal friend of his, to visit his recording studio in Athens, so what we have is a studio-quality recording, originally made in 1930. The music the duo played for Baud-Bovy were examples of village dance music, so we could expect a field recording made at this time to have had much more background noise.

This dance is performed by Manolis Niotis on the three-stringed, pear-shaped fiddle *lyra* and Komninos Papanikolaou on the long-necked, fretted lute *laouto*. These two instruments are a standard ensemble for the accompaniment of folk music from this region. The strings of the *lyra* are typically tuned to the notes g', d" and a" (a semitone sharper on the CD) and stopped with the fingernails. The fiddle rests on the musician's left thigh during seated performance, and is rotated to direct the bow from one string to another. The bow, until the 1930s, was short and curved, with attached bells adding rhythmic emphasis to the player's rapid right-hand movements. (Today, a straighter bow or violin bow may be used instead). Commonly, melodic patterns are played on the upper or middle string, with some performers adding a drone on either the lower or middle string as well (see page 80).

The *laouto* has eight strings, arranged as four pairs, again tuned in fifths (generally c, g, d' and a' – again, a semitone higher on the recording), and strummed with a plectrum (traditionally a quill from a goose feather). Although some *laouto* players at this time were beginning to add harmonized accompaniments, many others strummed chordal and rhythmic patterns appropriate to the nature of the dance they were accompanying. In some areas, *laouto* players preferred to strum a drone fifth on the lowest strings and perform a simplified imitation of the *lyra* melody on the higher strings.

The *sousta*

Meaning literally to 'spring', the *sousta* is an energetic circle dance in Karpathos. It is considered too rapid for simultaneous singing, but might be preceded or followed by slower dances where singing can take place. The dance is in simple duple time and has the characteristic rhythmic pattern: ♪♫♪♫ , most clearly heard in the *laouto* part of the recording.

Track 17

Sousta

The tune of this *sousta* employs a diatonic scale beginning on A♭, although the leading note (G) is very little used. Nonetheless, the tune is not harmonized in a tonal way. Instead, the *laouto* player repeats A♭ and E♭ (the two lowest pairs of strings) throughout as a drone. On top of this, he plays the same dance tune as the musician with the *lyra*. Overall then, the music has a heterophonic texture on top of a tonic and fifth drone.

This piece is primarily intended as dance music, perhaps leading one to expect regular phrase lengths. The excerpt in question does indeed have regular phrases (normally four bars). However, the phrases are combined in quite an inventive scheme, as shown below:

Section	Bars	Phrase	Comment (if any)
Introduction	1–12	i	rhythmic ostinato establishes dance speed and mood. Occasional B♭ in the *laouto* part adds further propulsion to the music.
A1	13–16	a	melody emphasizing notes of the tonic triad on strong beats: E♭–C–C–A♭
	17–20	a'	slightly varied repeat of phrase a
	21–24	a	
A2	25–28	b	contrasting melody, giving some stress to D♭ in its second bar but otherwise accenting A♭
	29–32	b	
	33–36	b'	altered cadence (to B♭)
B1	37–41	c'	third theme, again contrasting, with an outline of B♭ rising to D♭. One extra bar (37) makes five-bar phrase.
	42–45	d	answering phrase returning to B♭
	46–49	c	(c' without the extra bar)
	50–53	d	
B2	54–57	e	high register phrase, stressing F, E♭ and D♭
	58–61	d'	answering phrase, like phrase d except for its third bar
	62–65	e	
	66–69	d"	final bar adapted to cadence on A♭
C	70–73	f	phrase combining parts of earlier phrases (70=17, 71=62 [54], 72=44) to lead to E♭ cadence
	74–77	f'	adapted latter part to cadence back on A♭
	78–81	f	
	82–85	f'	
A3	86–97	b, b, b	much as before
	98–101	b'	
B3	102–118	c', d, c, d	much as before
Link	119+	i	much as before, linking to a shortened, adapted repeat of the whole dance

Note: all phrases have quaver upbeats

A *Lyra*

Cante Flamenco

Cultural background

Although *flamenco* is identified elsewhere as typically 'Spanish', within Spain it is associated with the southern province of Andalusia, and with the Spanish gypsies. The origin of the term *flamenco* is disputed, although in one explanation it is derived from 'flame', an idea which links *flamenco* to the aesthetic of a number of Middle Eastern vocal traditions. *Flamenco* itself comprises song (*cante*), dance and guitar music, and is performed in a wide range of situations, from the traditional, private *juerga* 'spree' to the concert hall and recording studio.

Whatever its exact origin, the performance of *cante flamenco* by gypsy musicians in southern Spain is documented for at least two centuries, and an essential event in the development of the style as we know it today was the opening in the mid-nineteenth century of *cafés cantantes*, places where groups gathered for nocturnal musical entertainment and alcohol. Apart from solo vocal performances, usually accompanied by the guitar, the practice also arose of group performances. In this style of performance, several singers take turns to provide the vocal part, again accompanied by one or two guitarists, with dance taking place simultaneously. In such performances today, castanets may be added, the result of quite recent influence of Spanish folk dance on the gypsies, who remain the principal, though not exclusive, performers of *flamenco* today.

Instrumentation

In this example, a male singer is accompanied by a *flamenco* guitar. Note the hoarse vocal quality employed. Apart from repeating chords and inserting short melodic passages, the guitarist also taps his fingers against a plate on the soundboard of the guitar, thus adding a percussive element to the texture. Others present may clap their hands, stamp their feet or call out cries of encouragement. The traditional mode of performance among a small group of friends encourages active participation from those not singing or playing the guitar.

The *bulerías*

Flamenco songs (and similarly dances and instrumental solos) are generally divided into three principal categories: the very intense, introverted *cante hondo*, or 'profound songs', the more moderate *cante intermedio* and the somewhat lighter *cante chico* type. The song transcribed is a typical example of the latter kind, one which relies upon a fast gypsy musical form, the *bulerías*.

Like many *flamenco* forms, the *bulerías* has a specific *compás*, or pattern of weak and strong beats used as a rhythmic cycle by the performers. The *compás* continues throughout the piece, possibly in varied or elaborated form. The *bulerías* has a *compás* of twelve beats with stress given to beats 3, 6, 8, 10 and 12. Patterns of hand-clapping or other accompanying rhythms may then be set across the basic stresses of the guitar, often resulting in great rhythmic complexity. A common means of combining a hand-clapping rhythm to the standard *bulerías* guitar part is shown below:

Guitar and Hand-Clapping Patterns in a *Bulerías*

This pattern may be further elaborated through the addition of more hand-claps, finger-snapping, stamps of the heel or the sounds of the dancers' feet. In each case, performers aim to exploit different sonorities and dynamic levels.

 *Track 18*

A mí no me gustan las rubias

The song partially transcribed, 'I Don't Like Blondes', is begun by a short guitar introduction (bars 1–4). This sets the mood and rhythmic style of the song. The singer begins by tuning in his voice with a sustained vocable, 'Ay' (bars 4–5). Typically, there may be several such phrases at the start of a *cante*. After a guitar interlude, during which an onlooker calls out to further encourage the singer, the vocalist re-enters with the first line of text (bars 7–8). Text is mostly sung in a syllabic style, and many lines in this performance are set to an arched contour, rising perhaps to E before falling back to the tonic pitch A. Generally, each line of text is separated by another instrumental interlude, some of which introduce variations to the opening rhythmic pattern or its harmonic base. Certain standardized guitar passages (*falsetas*) are memorized by *flamenco* accompanists and, like the singer's melodic arch, employed creatively during performance. Basic to song structure in this style is the maintenance of the rhythmic *compás*, with many songs comprising an additive structure of phrases of text linked by semi-related passages for guitar. Performers learn styles of performance, ornamentation and texts rather than set songs, and improvisation remains essential in *flamenco* performance, so the exact structure of a song can vary widely from one performance to another.

This *bulerías* uses a heptatonic scale beginning on A (transcribed a semitone above actual pitch), similar to the phrygian mode (A, B♭, C, D, E, F, G). The third degree of the scale appears both in natural (C) and raised (C♯) forms. The vocalist remains within the range of a fifth, from A to E. Certain vocal ornamentations are reserved for particular degrees of the scale. The guitar part, although primarily rhythmic in function, employs a handful of different chords, generally those of A major and B♭ major.

Summary-translation

[Ay] A mí no me gustan las rubias,
[Ay] Porque no saben besar.

[Ay] I don't like blondes,
[Ay] For they don't know how to kiss.

After continuing to describe the soothing nature of kisses from brunettes, the singer adds another stanza, in which he concludes that although each brunette is worth two blondes he will remain with the 'less expensive blonde of his heart'.

Fado Urban Song

Cultural background

Fado, literally 'fate', is probably the best known abroad of Portuguese traditional musical forms. It exists in two principal varieties, the *fado* of Lisbon and that of Coimbra. Both types of *fado* share a preference for texts which express nostalgia, sentimental love for an unobtainable woman, or longing. Both types appear to have developed primarily during the nineteenth century from a mixture of rural Portuguese and Afro-Brazilian styles with Italian *bel canto* operatic singing. Also, both are usually performed in restaurants and cafés. Nonetheless, there are important differences. In Coimbra, *fado* is closely associated with university life, students being amongst its principal practitioners. In Lisbon, on the other hand, a broader cross-section of society performs this song form and there are also more professional performers. Typically, Lisbon singers prefer an intense style of performance while those of Coimbra aim for a lyrical, restrained style.

A traditional *fado* consists of a text performed to one of a number of set musical outlines. This outline stipulates such features as the harmonic progressions to be used during the song, its melodic contour, the structure of each stanza of text, and accompaniment styles. During recent decades, however, many leading *fado* singers have created songs in *fado* style which do not strictly follow traditional frameworks.

Instrumentation

In *fado*, a solo voice is accompanied by a pair of plucked instruments: the *viola*, a form of guitar which traditionally has four or five strings, and the *guitarra portuguesa*, a long-necked lute related to the so-called English guitar with six double courses of strings. The *viola* provides the bass line and harmonic accompaniment of the *fado* while the *guitarra* is featured as a melodic instrument during interludes. Sometimes the player of the *guitarra portuguesa* improvises contrasting melodic passages to perform simultaneously with the vocal melody. Both these instruments rely predominantly upon traditional patterns, whether harmonic, rhythmic or melodic. These patterns, and the tuning of the instruments, differ somewhat from Lisbon to Coimbra. A form of bass guitar has more recently been added by some musicians, and studio versions scored for electronic or orchestral instruments are not unknown.

 *Track 19*

Maria Feia

Maria Feia, 'Plain Maria', is in strophic form and compound duple metre (6/8). Strophic form is unsurprising, but the use of 6/8 is somewhat unusual for a *fado*, most using 4/4 time. It may have resulted from the singer's adoption of a tune from local folk song. Reflecting the importance given to the text in *fado*, the words are clearly set, mostly in syllabic style.

Following an eleven-bar instrumental introduction there are three verses of text. Each verse uses the same music: four lines of text, a short instrumental interlude which harks bark to the end of the introduction, four more lines repeating the music of the first four lines, and a refrain. The refrain repeats the music of the introduction, with the melody now split between the *guitarra* and the singer, who sings to the syllable 'la'. In place of the refrain, the end of the third verse is modified to lead to a simple vocal cadenza on the dominant chord and two bars of instrumental tonic reiteration by way of a coda.

The song uses the tonality of D minor. Harmonies employed are primarily the root position chords of D minor, C major and A major, although B♭ major and F major also occur. This simple harmonic palette is typical of *fado* songs, especially the refrain section which alternates just two chords, D minor and C major.

Summary-translation

Eu naõ sei como te chamas,
    O Maria Feia,
Nem que nomo te hei de dôr,
    O Maria Feia, O Feia Maria, O Maria Feia, O Feia Maria.
Cravo naõ, que tu és rosa,
    O Maria Feia,
Rosa naõ, que naõ tem flor,
    O Maria Feia, O Feia Maria, O Maria Feia, O Feia Maria.
      [La, la, la, la, la, la, la.
      La, la, la, la, la, la, la.]

I don't know your name,
    O Maria Feia,
Nor which name I should give you,
    O Maria Feia, O Feia Maria, O Maria Feia, O Feia Maria.
Not carnation because you are a rose,
    O Maria Feia,
Not rose because it has no flower,
    O Maria Feia, O Feia Maria, O Maria Feia, O Feia Maria.
      [La, la, la etc.]

Two more verses follow in which the singer settles upon the image of a mirror as the right one for his love and declares his desolation without her.

Music for *Hardingfele*

Cultural background

Norwegian folk music has enjoyed a revival since the 1950s. Dying traditions have been resuscitated, old musicians documented and their music recorded. Revival has been a process of change as well as preservation, with fluid, regional fiddle styles like that of the *hardingfele* or Hardanger fiddle becoming emblems of national culture. Until quite recently, this instrument was performed only in rural areas of west and central Norway; in much of the rest of the country a trio or quartet of violins was preferred.

Hardingfele music consists mainly of songs and dances, some serving primarily as accompaniment pieces but others demanding careful listening. Performance is solo, the melody accompanied by the resonance of the sympathetic strings, occasional drones and the fiddler's regular foot-tapping. Melodies generally consist of short motifs which are continuously recycled in varied form during performance.

The *hardingfele*

Probably invented during the early seventeenth century, the *hardingfele* differs from the violin in having four or five sympathetic strings stretched beneath the fingerboard. Strings are metal, which increases the *hardingfele*'s volume. The fingerboard is short, musicians typically remaining in first position, and highly decorated. At the far end of the neck is a carved head, characteristically that of a horse, and the bridge is flat-topped to allow simultaneous bowing of melody and drone strings:

Sympathetic strings

The *Hardingfele*

Tuning and mode

A wide number of string tunings are employed on the *hardingfele*, but that recorded is most probably tuned as below:

Sample Tuning of the *Hardingfele*

Note: the lowest sympathetic string is not found on every *hardingfele*

The primary drone pitch in the transcribed piece is b', although the other three strings are sometimes sounded as drones as well. The heptatonic melody cadences at the halfway point and finally onto an E, and may thus be described by some as a lydian mode (E, F♯, G♯, A♯, B, C♯, D♯ and E). However, the *hardingfele* player envisages melodic material more in terms of sets of one open and four stopped notes per string. The fingers are normally put down at the same positions on all strings, so the following notes are available in the above tuning:

open string	index	middle	ring	little	(LH fingers)
f♯"	g♯"	a♯"	b"	c♯'''	
b'	c♯"	d♯"	e"	f♯"	
e'	f♯'	g♯'	a'	b'	
b	c♯'	d♯'	e'	f♯'	

Fingering Chart for *Hardingfele* (strings tuned as above)

A♮ is produced on the e' string (ring finger) while an octave higher A♯ is produced on the f♯" string (middle finger). Accordingly, low A♮ is as much a part of the mode of this piece as higher A♯.

Rhythm and metrical organization

Hardingfele music can be rhythmically complex. Against the musician's regular foot-beating (often in 3/8 time) are varying, syncopated melodic accents which arise from shifts between grouping two or three notes to each bow. Some dance tunes fluctuate between compound and simple duple time (6/8 and 2/4), and simple triple-time dances fairly commonly have one beat of each unit played a little faster than the other two. Finally, the end of one phrase may serve as the beginning of the next, so that metrical units overlap.

The recorded music is transcribed in 6/8 time, but 2/4, 3/4 and 9/8 would all have been more suitable for some passages. Metrical ambiguity is not resolved by the foot-beat which sustains a different, but regular, pattern of one short and two longer beats. It may be an example of the stately dance *gangar*, known for its overlapping phrases and use of hemiola, i.e. periodic switching from duple to triple time or the reverse. The complex melodic style suggests that this performance is intended primarily for listening, not dance.

Scholars have paid much attention to the question of rhythm and metrical organization in *hardingfele* music. According to some, the rhythmic structure of the fiddler's foot-beating and bowing reflects the steps, stretches and turns of the dancers. Others argue that there are three simultaneous metres (foot-beat, melody and bow) which fit into a regular, large-scale rhythmic cycle. Research on foreign musicians suggests that they make sense of *hardingfele* rhythms through the filter of their own experience. Those who expect music to have a single, clear metre hear syncopated, ambiguous or confusing music, those accustomed to more complex metrical structures experience extended, multi-beat metrical patterns, and those familiar with the simultaneous performance of different metres listen to this music as polymetric.

 *Track 20*

Svein I Sy' Garde

'The Boy on his Farm' has a sectional form, each section consisting of the repetition and development of a small number of short melodic patterns. There are three basic motifs in this piece, each of which has a contrasting melodic style and pattern of string use:

Bars	Section	Comments
1–10	1	melody played on f♯" (top) string accompanied by drone on adjacent b' string occasionally punctuated by touch on e' string. Melodic motifs include B–B–A♯–C♯–B, F♯–G♯–A♯–B and B–B–G♯–B–A♯.
11–20	2	'opposite' pattern: melody now on b' string and decorated drone (G♯–F♯) on f♯" string. Much playing in parallel fifths (f♯" and b' strings bowed and fingered simultaneously) with melodic C♯–B patterns paralleled by G♯–F♯. Note hemiola rhythms: (1) within beats – compare, for example, bar 16^2 and bar 17^1; (2) metrical displacement – patterns in whole section are nine quavers long (count back from the end of bar 20, noting repeats).
21–26	3	drone on b' string (sometimes replaced with c♯" or d♯") played above falling-contour motif on e' string starting on A♮. Once interrupted by a shift up a string (bar 25). Hemiola patterns in melody and phrase structure continue.
27–29	2	repeat of 18–20, slightly varied.
30–36	3	repeat of 21–26, varied. Drone character of upper part clearer. Lowest string occasionally sounded (d♯'s in bars 31–32).
36–39	2	repeat of 18–20, again slightly varied.
39–44	3	repeat of 21–26, varied. Falling melodic contour adapted to lead to cadence onto E.

The whole pattern is then repeated, in developed form, with motifs 2 and 3 played just twice.

Lullaby

Cultural background   Norwegian vocal forms include composed church, school and art music as well as several types of folk song. Amongst the latter, herding songs, religious tunes, ballads and lullabies were once widely popular. Some of these now exist only on museum recordings, but others are maintained in the new context of the folk music concert, as well as in their more traditional settings. One such example is the lullaby, or *bånsull*.

As might be expected from consideration of its main apparent function, the Norwegian lullaby restricts itself to a narrow melodic range, a small number of melodic ingredients and a soft dynamic level. No instrumental accompaniment is used. Text is clearly set, with just one or two notes to most syllables. These repetitive songs are easy to memorize, but the simple melody and repetition of a refrain between each short verse also allows a singer to extend a song by improvising new verses during performance.

Lullabies may have functions quite apart from the lulling of babies to sleep. Some are effectively initial counting or naming lists, which introduce the baby to specific objects, shapes or quantities. Also, the emotional bond of infant to parent may be strengthened by the effect of the parent's voice on the baby. Thirdly, in societies where male and female roles are strictly demarcated and child-rearing is seen as a female occupation, a woman with little direct say in the running of her own household can use the lullaby to offer advice, criticize her husband or other relatives, request the purchase of particular items, or bemoan some aspect of her existence. Although the song is addressed to the (seemingly) uncomprehending baby, it is sung at a time when the woman knows she will be overheard by those whom she wishes to influence. As such, these lullabies, with words newly improvised to suit each new occasion, are a form of domestic protest song. Finally, in such societies, the uninterfered-with singing of such complaints can have a calming effect upon the singer herself.

   *Track 21*   *Bånsull*

This lullaby is sung unaccompanied in simple quadruple metre. The final syllable of the second line of the verse and the refrain is sustained for an extra beat, giving, in effect, a 5/4 bar at these points. There are two structural elements, a verse segment and a refrain segment. Both verse and lullaby use closely related melodic material, although it is differently combined in each:

Bars	Phrase	Segment	Cadence Note
0–2	**A**	Verse	G
3–4	**B**		B
4–6	**A**		G
7–8	**A**	Refrain	G
9–10	**B'**		E

The whole structure is then repeated, with a new text set to the verse segment.

In modal terms, the lullaby uses a hexatonic (six-note) scale with E as fundamental: E, F♯, G, A, B and D♯. B is of secondary importance, beginning many phrases and providing the contrasting cadence at bar 4. G is also significant, with several phrases ending on this note. A, D♯ and F♯ are the less important, with A occurring only in a single melodic pattern where it decorates movement from high B down to G. D♯ is found only as a decoration of an adjacent E, while F♯ is used either as an upper auxiliary ornamentation of E or as a lower approach to a cadential G. To listeners familiar with the scales of Western art music, the weighting of E, G and B will suggest the key of E minor, an impression supported by the use of D♯ in the melody. However, in a very typical E minor piece, there would be some differences. For example, we might expect the D♯–E step at the end of bar 1 to be followed by another step to F♯ at the start of bar 2, not a leap to G or the D♯ in bar 4 to be followed either by a return to E or by a C♯.

Summary-translation

The lullaby is sung in a regional dialect of Norwegian and includes certain archaic words. The two verses shown on the transcription appear to be an excerpt from a longer song about a fox and a baby. Each verse mentions a part of the face and suggests a humorous use for it. One can perhaps imagine the singer touching a new part of the baby's face during each verse.

Inuit Throat-Singing

Cultural background

The Inuit inhabit an extensive area around the rim of the Arctic Ocean, with widely-scattered, small communities found in Russia, Alaska, Canada and Greenland. Commonly referred to as 'Eskimo', the term is actually disparaging, meaning 'eaters of raw meat'. There is no specific word in traditional Inuit language for 'music', but based on what Inuit people actually do we can describe Inuit musical activity as consisting primarily of songs and dance-songs accompanied by drumming. Some of these are performed as duels, with each singer attempting to shame his adversary, either to settle a dispute or to publicly vent anger in a non-destructive way. Other songs and dances have ritual use, praising or questioning the spirits, marking the exchange of presents or launching of a boat, and preceding hunting missions. Certain songs employ texts consisting partly or wholly of meaningless syllables, or 'vocables'. There are children's songs and a range of entertainment music. In recent years, Inuit musicians have also adopted and adapted various European and North American musical instruments and styles.

Despite the great distance and relative isolation of one community from another, Inuit music-making shares a number of general characteristics, such as the use of repeated rhythmic patterns performed on a frame drum to accompany singing and dance. Other musical aspects are more specific to certain regions. An example is *katajjaq*, a vocal game normally sung by pairs of women sitting close and face to face, which is now performed primarily by Canadian Inuit. *Katajjaq* raises the question for the non-Inuit musician of whether it is a form of musical performance, since sound resources are performed through time; or is it simply a type of competitive sport, as the Inuit might say? Even though this may be a game for the Inuit, could we enjoy it as a kind of musical performance event ourselves? Such questions reveal something of our own cultural preconceptions about music.

Katajjaq

Unlike some of the longer ritual songs, which are carefully structured, composed and rehearsed tellings of myths or reminiscences of the significant events of a singer's life, *katajjaq* performances are typically short bursts of sound activity improvised during performance. The two participants squat with their mouths only a few centimetres apart, and attempt to set up a synchronized, interlocking pattern of voiced and unvoiced sounds. These sounds range from audible panting noises to vocables and, in some regions, from simple texts to archaic words or the imitation of animal sounds. Once synchronization has been established, the performers increase the speed of their patterns, until one or other of them breaks down or runs out of breath. Since it is tiring to maintain these patterns for long, it is rare for a performance to last more than thirty seconds, although several different games may be strung one after another with short breaks in between.

Katajjaq performances take place under a number of circumstances, often in the context of recreation, but sometimes to bid a visitor welcome or farewell or celebrate a successful hunt. One of the singers chooses the rhythmic patterns, and the pair agree how many times each motif should be repeated. Old women teach children how to pronounce, intone and co-ordinate their rhythmic elements clearly. As with Inuit song duels, skilled exponents gain prestige both for themselves and for their settlements.

Katajjaq performance

There is no set or predetermined structure to a *katajjaq* performance, other than the repetition of short rhythmic patterns over and over at a gradually increasing speed. Some contests switch from one set of sounds to another during mid-course, providing a multiple-section structure, but all throat-games are very short in duration. Of the three excerpts transcribed, one is a warm-up exercise in which one singer performs three patterns ending with repetition of the first (structure: **A B C A**) whilst the other maintains the same pattern throughout. The second and third are more typical competitive chants, one involving two rhythmic patterns (**A B**), the other having two very closely related patterns alternated by one competitor (**A B A B A B A**) whilst the other employs a single type.

Mode or pitch may be irrelevant, with changes in pitch being a consequence of the sound patterns chosen by each vocalist rather than an intentional compositional feature. Likewise, there is no overall metrical structure, although the specific rhythm of the text, vocables or breathing noises employed may pattern the resulting sounds.

Inuit Solo Song

Cultural background

In the study of Western classical music it is traditional to give great attention to the lives and personalities of individual composers. Presumably, we believe that understanding the creator of the music will help us to understand the music itself. However, when ethnomusicologists began to investigate the music of other cultures they often held a different point of view. Instead of trying to explain musical pieces that were already well-known, their hope was to discover broader cultural and human trends in music, and they looked more at groups and societies than at individual musicians. The music and musicians they studied, it was thought, should be representative of the culture as a whole, not idiosyncratic. As a result, individual aspects of music-making around the world were not strongly emphasized. Composition was described as an anonymous process, with new pieces and songs gradually shaped by an unknown mass of creators.

This particular view seems to be one shared by the original recorder of the song example studied below, or at least by the editor of the CD upon which it is issued. Although many songs on this CD have brief biographical details (performer's name, occupation and age), the information given most weight seems to be the location of the recording session and the dates when the recordist visited that area. For example, introducing a set of seven songs, the recordist uses seven sentences to tell us: the name of the settlement and its geographical location (Iglulik, north-west Canada); the months within which he made these recordings (in 1960–61); how many Inuit live in this settlement (600), and what their principal occupations are (hunting seals and walrus); the name and dates of the first Western explorer to visit this community, and his achievements; that one of the seven songs is sung whilst waiting for a seal to emerge at a breathing hole in the ice; its singer's name, age and occupation; and the fact that the recordist sometimes travelled by dog-sled on research with this man.

The idea that foreign people are simply representatives of their particular race or culture is now losing ground, and many ethnomusicologists are aware of the special role played by inventive musical individuals in each society. But until this trend (and the publication of its results) becomes more widespread, music teachers will not be able to ask the same kind of questions of world musics that they can with more familiar repertories.

For instance, we are unable to investigate the reasons behind the creation or singing of this song, and we do not have any idea about its intended use or actual function. Of course, even though we know nothing about this song, its recorded sound remains the same. Yet, whilst listening to it, perhaps we should consider whether we would hear it differently if we knew it was a love song, a lullaby, a ritual recitation or perhaps a chant performed to occupy dull moments when hunting. Quite likely it is one of the latter, since it sounds similar to several more clearly identified examples of such songs. But even if, by educated guesswork, we think this is a hunting song, we would still benefit from knowing something about the aims and values of the composer and performer as they relate to this particular song. By what process was it created, and how conscious is the composer of the structural outline of this song? Is it a pre-existent outline which he is re-using in his own way, in which case what makes this song different from others based on the same structure? Or has the composer, by combining traditional or newly-created elements, come up with a new song structure? If we could answer questions such as these, then it would be possible to begin teaching non-Western musics in the same ways that we study Western classical and popular pieces. This would be beneficial because it would remind us that no one musical tradition is any more unique than the others. Each is the product of a particular collection of human individuals, responding to a unique blend of historical, cultural, social and personal influences.

② Track 23

Solo song

Analysis of this song reveals several interesting features. It employs a pentatonic scale (E, F♯, G♯, B and C♯ – but a semitone lower at the beginning, while the singer warms up). The song consists of a series of lines, each one based on the same plan. In the recorded excerpt we hear six complete lines. There are two phrases to each line, the first beginning on B and cadencing on F♯, the second sliding back up to B and cadencing on E. These three notes are the most important ones, G♯ and C♯ being used less often. Each phrase can be subdivided into a number of elements (shown by dotted barlines on the transcription).

The first phrase has two elements: the first partially melismatic with an undulating melody falling from B to F♯, and the second with several syllables reiterated on the note F♯. The text of the first element, which is identical in each line, appears to be entirely composed of the vowel sounds 'Ae', 'yai' and 'ya'. Rhythmically, too, this element holds its pattern in each line, although occasionally the final note is elongated. In the second element there is a different text for each line, and these seem to be actual words rather than vocables. Rhythmically, there is a bit of variety from one line to another.

In the second phrase of each line there are three elements. The first takes up the undulating melodic style of the beginning of the first phrase, but this time combined with text rather than vocables. In fact, it repeats and continues the actual text of the previous element. Rhythmically and melodically, this element shows some variation as the song progresses, but its main details remain constant. The second element of phrase 2 is more regular, always comprising eight short-length notes: four repeated Es followed by a scale down from G♯. The style is syllabic, using actual words until the final note or two, which are given vocables. The third element is the simplest in the whole song, typically consisting of vowels like those at the start, set to three medium-length Es.

Repetition of each line gives us a ready sense of the overall shape of the song. Within each line there is a blend of repetition and variety. The cadencing of phrases to F♯ and E respectively supplies further patterned contrast and a consistent tonal scheme. Melodic variety is provided within each phrase by the alternation of undulating melodic segments and repeated notes, and by the alternation of strictly repeated segments with more freely varied ones. Rhythmic interest is maintained by the occasional use of medium-duration notes, and by the contrast of melisma with strict, syllabic text-setting.

For reasons such as these, the song may sound satisfying to us as listeners even though we cannot understand the text. Given access to the thoughts of the original composer, however, we could still appreciate these aspects of the music while also discovering what makes this song a special and individual example of Inuit music, not simply an exemplar of it.

Sioux Indian Song

Cultural background

American Indian music is amongst the best documented traditional musical styles world-wide. Nonetheless, this music is little heard outside the United States, or indeed by non-Indian listeners there, except in Hollywoodesque imitations. Generally, American Indian music varies from one area to another, but some forms, such as Plains Indian dance songs, are known by many Indians all over America.

Features common to much traditional Indian music-making include the widespread use of vocables ('meaningless' syllables). Songs are often composed of a few phrases and sections, which are repeated several times in varied form before a final coda. Apparently, slightly varied repetition is more highly valued in the American Indian aesthetic than complete originality. Certain songs are performed as solo calls with group response; in these, solo and group sections may overlap slightly. Few melodic instruments are employed, although many varieties of rattle and drum can be heard accompanying voices. Occasionally, a solo flute, whistle, musical bow or fiddle are heard, but there is no history of instrumental ensemble performance. Today, American Indians take part in a wide range of musical activities, from country-and-western-style popular music to modern school and church songs, and from traditional ceremonial songs to lullabies and dances. The remainder of this description concentrates on the more traditional portion of this repertory.

In traditional Native American society, music and dance accompanied a wide range of activities. Amongst these are ritual chants for purification, sung prayers, healing songs, songs used in courtship, gift songs, songs sung at times of war, hunting songs, praise songs directed at the chief and dream songs sung by members of particular societies. Ceremonies include those where members of several tribes meet (powwows), and here singing and dancing may develop a competitive edge, with prizes being awarded to the best performers. Other traditional situations that often called for music included begging, the telling of legends, and children's play. Composition as a musical skill was supplemented by the receipt by singers of songs in dreams and visions, especially the more important ceremonial songs. Other songs were simply borrowed from neighbouring Indian groups.

Sioux song

The Sioux (or Dakota) were traditionally inhabitants of a central northern part of the United States (North and South Dakota and contiguous areas), and are representative of the Northern Plains Indians. Amongst the general characteristics displayed in much of this region's traditional music are: a preference for descending melodies, perhaps beginning in falsetto and falling over a range of more than an octave; the use of a tense vocal quality; a reliance upon strophic structures, although repetition may be only partial; the employment of relatively complex rhythmic patterns and strong emphases; the avoidance of a single, simple metrical structure; the relative rhythmic independence of the drum accompaniment, if any; and the marking of phrase-ends with descending vocal slides. As in Native American music in general, the performance of songs with repetitive lyrics of vocables is common.

 *Track 24*

Sioux Flag Song

This song shows the influence of the Euro-Americans upon the Sioux, both in the content of its text (see below) and because it acts as a form of national anthem for the Sioux. As such, it is performed on ceremonial occasions, such as the opening of a powwow, without any dance. Nonetheless, it still demonstrates many of the features of traditional Native American music listed above. Despite the upward leaps at the start of most phrases, the melody follows a predominantly descending contour; it begins in falsetto, produced with a tightly constricted throat; phrase ends are often marked by falling vocal slides; and a strophic structure is used. In this case, a verse of text follows a verse of vocables, both of which are then repeated. Similarly, the drum rhythm does not closely follow the vocal part.

Transcribed in compound triple time, the vocal melody does not fall into a strict and regular pattern throughout. However, some phrases, especially in the first part of the song, are of regular length. Until almost the end, the drum merely reiterates (fairly) regular beats, some of which coincide with the start of vocal phrases. Although these drum beats are regular, they are not weighted to give a sense of relative strong and weak beats. The men, of whom there are six, sing primarily in heterophonic style, although the song opens with a solo voice and contains other passages performed by fewer singers.

No specific theory of mode is articulated by the Sioux Indians. In this particular example, the pitches used are G♯, A♯, B, C♯ and D♯. Technically, this is a pentatonic scale (with G♯ as fundamental). However, A♯ is only used in the higher register and is always placed between two occurrences of G♯, so it may be more accurate to consider this predominantly a four-note musical composition.

Summary-translation

Only the second section of this song contains lexical words. Freely translated, these apparently read: 'The President's flag will stand forever. Under it, the people will grow, so I will do this.'

Texas Folk Song

Cultural background

There are many traditions of folk music in the United States, reflecting the diverse origins of its present population. These traditions are sustained and developed by some during their daily lives, and employed by others as useful tools solidifying the identity of particular racial or social groups. Still other Americans study folk musical traditions as an aspect of their national history which reveals something of the flavour of life in earlier generations not readily shown by more formal historical sources. Music scholars have traced many of the texts and tunes employed by English-speaking white settlers back to English, Scottish and Irish progenitors. However, these verses and melodies were often adapted by the new Americans. The hero of a folk song in land-locked Texas, for instance, might become a cowboy rather a sailor, and singers developed personal versions of favoured songs. Also, in contact with vocal traditions from Negro spirituals to Spanish song and exposed to quite new social contexts, English-speaking folk musicians in the Southern part of the United States were stimulated to create and blend styles in ways their British counterparts never imagined.

Track 25

Godamighty Drag

The song transcribed and recorded is performed by a solo singer accompanied by a guitarist, and is an example of a work song from a Texas prison farm. It has nine verses in all (the first four are transcribed), and tells the story of a prisoner who laments the length of his stay in prison. The final two verses repeat the words of verses 1 and 2, although the singer hums the last few lines to conclude the song.

In common with many work songs, this one could be sung by a team of singers, with phrases being given alternately to leader and chorus, in antiphonal style. In a group performance, the leader can think up extra verses while the chorus repeats one or two simple phrases. Unlike some work songs, however, the vocal part of this one does not have an energetically rhythmic character.

Instead, with its gentle swing, it may have been intended more to maintain the spirits of the workers during their enforced labour than to synchronize manual activity.

Godamighty Drag is in moderate common time and the key of E major. Its accompaniment uses three chords: E major, A major and B7. The melody occupies a baritone register, from low B to e', and features voice slides and grace notes as standard forms of ornamentation. Each phrase moves from the third or fourth beat of one bar to the second or third of the next, with eight such phrases constituting a verse. Text-phrases are repeated in the pattern: a, b, a, b', c, b, c, b'.

Cantometrics

The singer on this recording is not a Texan prisoner, but a folklorist named Alan Lomax. Lomax has collected and studied folk songs from around the world, but especially from his native United States. Part of his work has been to promote greater respect for traditional music, and to do this Lomax devised a system of listening to music called 'cantometrics'. This consists, in part, of a very carefully compiled set of folk song recordings and an extensive list of stylistic attributes from which each recording could be assessed. Through using this system, listeners are able to compare the specific technical characteristics of different folk song styles.

Among the features that Lomax incorporated in his song-scale were such as accent, rasp, nasality, enunciation, glottal ornamentation, melisma, glissando, tremolo, rubato, embellishment, polyphonic type and interval size. A scale of numbers was given for each, and by circling that appropriate to the recorded song the listener arrives at a kind of 'voice-print' of the style in question. Different voice-prints could then be compared to reach conclusions about different musical styles. There have been many criticisms of this idea, particularly as to whether a single example can really be expected to show all that is typical or significant of a specific musical culture. If not, comparison may not be entirely worthwhile. However, as far as heightening listener sensitivity to the varied characteristics of vocal music from around the world is concerned, the cantometrics system has many strengths. In all, Lomax lists thirty-seven features, amongst which are those shown below:

1) Phrase length	1		4		7		10		13
2) No. of phrases	1	3	5	6		8	9	11	13
3) Range	1		4		7		10		13
4) Interval width	1		4		7		10		13
5) Embellishment	1		4		7		10		13
6) Tempo	1	3	5			9		11	13
7) Rubato	1		5			9			13
8) Glissando	1		5			9			13
9) Melisma	1				7				13
10) Tremolo	1				7				13
11) Glottal shake	1				7				13
12) Nasality	1		4		7		10		13
13) Raspiness	1		4		7		10		13
14) Accent	1		4		7		10		13
15) Enunciation	1		4		7		10		13

Illustration of Alan Lomax's Cantometrics System

Instructions:
Circle the value (or values) most appropriate to the recorded example. Generally, a low number means none or very little of the feature in question, while a score of 13 means this feature is present throughout or very marked. In the case of tempo, the greater the speed the higher the score; likewise for aspects such as interval width, phrase length, number of phrases and range. Join the circles with a line and use the resulting graph as an aid in comparing different songs.

Music for Steel Band

Cultural background

Trinidadian steel band music is a highly eclectic form which retains elements from African and Hispanic music, combined with British and French influences. Recognized as an indigenous form in contemporary Trinidad, the influence of steel band has extended across the entire Caribbean region and beyond. The nature of this music reflects the history of the island and its population. Indigenous Arawak Indians died out during Spanish colonial rule (1498–1797), while under subsequent British rule slaves were brought from West Africa and then labourers from East India to work in the sugar-cane fields and refineries. The mixed ethnic composition, different cultural backgrounds, languages and religions introduced by the immigrants have produced a unique national culture and a great variety of musical forms, such as the steel band and calypso music.

Calypso music

Calypso is essentially an urban form. Its lyrics serve an important social function, reflecting and commenting upon personal, social and economic problems or satirizing current political events. This social function may be evidence of its West African heritage, as also may be the use of call and response structures. The rhythm of calypso may be said to be Afro-Hispanic, being similar to the metrical structures of Brazilian *samba*, whilst the melodies tend to be European-derived. There is a common fund of about fifty melodies which are used, re-used, altered, re-altered and continually set to new texts. Many tunes are in a major key modulating to the dominant, but some alternate between tonic major and minor.

Calypso is thought to have originated in the Carnival of Port of Spain, Trinidad's capital. In the eighteenth century, this festival was mainly celebrated as a religious holiday by the ruling Europeans. However, following emancipation, it was adopted by the newly-freed slaves and transformed into a lively occasion. Raucous songs were sung, accompanied by West African and East Indian percussion instruments. In 1884, the use of African drums in street processions was banned by the white ruling classes, who hoped to suppress the sentiments surrounding the Carnival. This forced the musicians to look for other kinds of instruments and, after developing bands of struck bamboo tubes, they took in the latter part of the 1940s to fashioning tuned idiophones from oil drums. With their extended range and versatility, these 'pans' quickly replaced the older bamboo instruments and steel band performances, no longer restricted to the annual Carnival, attract listeners from all over the world.

Instrumentation

Pitch, tuning, note-layout and nomenclature are not standardized, so the following description may not suit every steel band. There are three basic categories of pan. The first, tenor pans (or ping pongs) play the melody and have a range of up to two octaves, though they may not be entirely chromatic. The second category are the rhythm pans (also known as guitar pans, second pans and cello pans). These are lower in pitch, and play a supporting role over a range of about an octave. The third category of instrument are the bass pans (or tuned booms), which have a range of three or five notes and provide the lowest pitches. By using multiple instruments in each category, a fully chromatic range over a wide register and a thick texture result. All these pans are played with rubber-headed sticks. Modern steel bands also include drum kit, vibraphone, congas, bongos and other percussion.

Soulful Calypso

This simple duple time composition has two parts, each repeated, which alternate in a simple **A A B B** form. The excerpt recorded and transcribed comes from the middle of a longer performance and includes two statements of section **A**, two of **B**, two more of **A** and two more of **B**. Each rendition of section **A** consists of a sixteen-bar theme beginning in the middle register. Section **B**, which begins in the upper register, is shorter than **A**. Its first statement is eight bars in length. In place of the final two-bar cadential pattern, the second statement is extended by a short linking passage before the return to section **A**. Harmonically, section **A** is a little more complex than section **B**, using triads of D major (the tonic), A (the dominant), A7, G major and E minor. Section **B** uses only the chords of D and A.

The melody is based around the notes of the triad, with some stepwise motion for decoration. The rhythmic style of this example is typically syncopated, especially in section **B** and among the centrally-pitched rhythm pans. Also contributing to this rhythmic affect are the bass drum, shaker and cowbells, all performed in a style reminiscent of Brazilian *samba* percussion.

Colombia

Dance for *Chirimía* Ensemble

Cultural background Colombia is located at the northern end of South America, bordering Panama, Venezuela, Brazil, Peru and Ecuador. In the past, it was part of the Inca Empire, overthrown by Spanish conquerors in 1533. The Spaniards and Portuguese brought African slaves to coastal areas, and European settlers also established their own communities. Referring to the three main races inhabiting the continent, it is commonly stated that music in South America is a blend of Indian, African and Iberian elements. There is some truth in this, but of course not all South American music reflects all three of these influences. Nor were there ever single Indian, African or Iberian musical styles. The music of some groups today has more in common with that of specific South American Indian cultures, other music exhibits primarily European features, some music closely resembles distinct African models, and certain compositions fuse two of these elements.

In Colombia, West African influence, strongest in the Pacific coastal region, is reflected in features such as the solo call and group response structure with tonic–dominant tonal alternation, polymetric musical organization, interlocking rhythmic patterns, dance styles and instruments. Spanish elements include the preservation of archaic styles of Spanish folk music and the proliferation of small, guitar-like instruments. Indian elements, found especially in southern Colombia, include a preference for instrumental combinations such as flutes and drums, set rhythmic patterns and the preservation of earlier musical practices at the rural festivals held during the religious and agricultural year. The transcribed example comes from an Colombian Indian community.

Traditionally, many of the South American Indian peoples believed musical instruments to be of great symbolic significance and ritual power. For example, owing to their phallic shape, many varieties of flute were reserved for male performers. A second symbolic instrument was the slit drum, made from a hollowed log and performed with a single beater, an instrument which represented female–male dualism. Another ritual instrument is the rattle, the sound of which was thought to reflect the voices of spirits, and to call spirits to a shaman.

The *chirimía* ensemble

Chirimía is the name of a small, traditional Spanish reed instrument, but in Colombia it can refer to a number of different instrumental ensembles used to accompany singing or dancing. In the Pacific coastal region, where it is believed this ensemble originated, a typical group consists of clarinet (replacing the older *chirimía*), two double-headed drums (one large, one small) and locally-made cymbals. In the Andean region, two or three transverse flutes replace the clarinets, and maracas and a rasp replace the cymbals. The employment of flutes, rather than clarinets, is the result of indigenous Indian inclinations. In the transcribed example, four transverse flutes (themselves called *chirimías*) perform the melody, accompanied by a *guacharaca* rasp – a notched piece of wood, cane or gourd scraped with a stick, nail or metal fork – and a *tambora* two-headed drum, which is struck with a mallet and either a stick or the bare hand.

Track 27

Viejo Miguel

'Old Miguel' is performed by a *chirimía* ensemble of Indian musicians from southern Colombia to accompany a fast dance performed on festive occasions. Often, such music does not have a specific title but is named after the primary event where it takes place. The performers remind themselves of old pieces and compose new ones by rehearsing collectively a few days before each event.

There are three themes, each repeated several times. Theme **A** has two phrases, the second an adaptation of the first. It exploits the upper range of the *chirimía*, beginning with a leap to the tonic note F (transcribed a semitone below actual pitch) and gradually falling to the dominant C. Theme **B**, constructed from four short phrases, continues this overall falling contour: its first phrase falls to the third of the scale, A, the second reaches G, the third rises again to the dominant and the final phrase cadences on the lower tonic. These themes are doubled a parallel third lower, a feature common to Spanish, West African and South American Indian traditional musics. Theme **C** alternates the leading note (a step lower than **B**'s final cadence note) and the tonic, adding decorative up-beat arpeggio patterns and answering descending parallel thirds. In a tonal sense, this theme acts more as a coda or refrain, reinforcing the tonal emphasis reached at the end of theme **B**. In texture, however, it differs from the earlier homophonic themes in employing a solo melody with responding (antiphonal) parallel thirds. These themes are ordered in a structure of two verses each followed by a refrain:

Bars	Section	Themes
1–12	verse 1	**A, B, B**
12–22	refrain	**C, C, C, C, C**
22–38	verse 2	**A, A, B, B**
38–46	refrain	**C, C, C, C**

The dance uses a diatonic major scale, probably the result of European influence, and quadruple time. There is no use of percussion polyrhythms. Instead, the percussion instruments mostly maintain a long–short–short rhythmic pattern throughout. Sometimes, however, this pattern sounds closer to that of three notes of equal duration.

Kuli Panpipe Ensemble

Cultural background

The example of Colombian *kuli* panpipe ensemble music transcribed and recorded comes from the Cunas Indians of northern Colombia, a people which inhabit regions of Panama also. The *kuli* is just one of their panpipe-type instruments, and is not as important in Cunas cultural life as the larger instrument, the *kamul-purui*. The *kamul-purui* consists of seven or eight pipes bound in two groups. One set of pipes is known as the female, the other as the male, and they are sounded alternately. The *kuli* is thought to be the predecessor of the *kamul-purui*. It is simpler in design, consisting of only one tube or a pair. Again, if there is a pair, they are played alternately. Like the larger panpipe, an ensemble of differently-tuned *kuli* may be used to produce more elaborate melodies and musical effects.

Ritual musical life among the Cunas Indians is overseen by a pair of specialists. The *kantule* has the duty of remembering the traditional tunes and teaching them to the rest of the tribe when required. In this he is assisted by the *kansueti*, who carefully cuts bamboo to make new instruments for the performers.

The *kuli* ensemble

In the ensemble transcribed there are three performers. One of them plays a single tube tuned approximately to the note A. The second plays two tubes, roughly equivalent to G and F. The third performer also plays two *kuli*, and these are tuned to pitches close to D and C. In the case of the pairs, the higher note is known as the female one. To sound the tubes, the players blow over the upper edge of the bamboo pipe.

By performing in hocket fashion (i.e. like hand-bell ringers) the three musicians can produce a pentatonic melody. However, they also play in combination, producing chords and clusters of notes. Finally, the musicians vary the performance by using their voices and by striking or rubbing the instruments together in a percussive way.

 *Track 28*

Structure

Kuli performance

No title is given for the short performance recorded. It has four elements in all, and demonstrates an overall ternary form. The first element consists of the musicians blowing their pipes alternately. They do this in a set pattern: first player, second player (both pipes) and third player (both pipes). Since there are five pipes and each one is blown for approximately the same amount of time, this passage has a five-beat feel. One additional feature of interest is that although the second musician always blows his pipes F then G, the third player alternates between playing C–D in one bar and D–C in the next. Two-bar-long alternation of patterns like this is a feature of the whole composition. They repeat this pattern many times until the third player cues the beginning of the next element of the composition.

The second element consists of all three blowing fast repeated notes together. After sixteen notes, the second and third *kuli* players quickly switch from lower to higher pipe. Again, they play sixteen fast notes. Like the first element, the whole pattern is repeated.

The third element is very closely related to the second, using the same rhythmic pattern. However, instead of playing, the musicians call out 'Ha-ha-ha-ha'. Gradually, their voices fall in pitch and volume. After this pattern has been repeated vocally, it is re-orchestrated and reproduced as percussive, bamboo clicking sounds, the fourth element of this music. The fourth element is repeated, and then the musicians return to the opening.

To complete the performance they repeat the first two elements, although the repeat is not strict. Overall, this gives a ternary shape to the music, although the central material (elements 3 and 4) is closely related to that of element 2 in rhythm and style. The structure of the music is summarized below:

Bars	Section	Element	Metre and Rhythm
1–11	A	1	5/4 – five even notes to each phrase, except the last which has one beat less
12–16		2	4/2 – sets of up to sixteen, repeated fast notes
17–20	B	3	4/2 – the repeated fast notes continue. The last bar has one beat less.
21–24		4	4/2 and 3/2 – still repeated notes, and the shortened last bar
25–35	A	1	5/4 – largely as before
36–40		2	4/2 – largely as before, with adapted ending

Brazil

Ritual Dance-Song Rehearsal

Cultural background

So many cultures and sub-cultures constitute the modern nation of Brazil that it would be impossible to provide a single, definitive example of Brazilian music. Affluent and urban areas may prefer European and American styles of music, whether classical, jazz or popular, while African-derived traditions are actively maintained elsewhere and, in the interior, many indigenous styles have evolved. Needless to say, there are also many mixed musical traditions. The example selected is a single aspect of the music-making of one of the indigenous peoples, the Kaiapó Indians.

The Kaiapó Indian tribes inhabit more than a dozen small villages scattered along the banks of tributaries of the Xingu River in south-east Pará and north-east Mato Grosso. This area is an extensive transitional zone between regions of dense rain forest and open grassland. Kaiapó villages are laid out in a very formal way, and the relationship between space and social role is of great significance to them. Each village consists of a circle of regularly-spaced living huts arranged around a spacious clearing. In the middle of this is the men's house. It is in this central space that village rituals and public affairs take place, and the men take a leading role in these. The women live around the edge of the village, growing crops in gardens and gathering wood and wild food from the forest. The men occupy themselves outside the village with hunting in the forest and fishing.

Kaiapó music

Kaiapó music is predominantly vocal, although a few instruments such as rattles, flutes and horns are sometimes employed for accompaniment and signalling. Much Kaiapó music is bound up with ceremonial activity. Situations such as naming ceremonies, agricultural, hunting and fishing rites, and rituals performed on occasions such as eclipses are all accompanied by singing and dancing. Musical performances at these events are carefully prepared for with several weeks of rehearsal, which allow the younger men to memorize song texts. In ritual performance the men sing in high voices or 'falsetto', whereas in rehearsal they pitch their voices much lower.

The corn ceremony

The most important of the Kaiapó's agricultural rituals is the corn ceremony. Corn is the Kaiapó's staple diet during the months of the rainy season. Seeds are planted at the end of the dry season in September or October, and the ceremony begins two months later. Essential to the corn ceremony are three dances performed by the adult men to stimulate growth of the plants and ensure a good harvest. Each night-long dance is preceded by a month of rehearsal and expeditions to gather food and costuming materials. The final dance is the *no'ok-'a mor*, a dance in which the men make up their faces with paint.

 *Track 29*

No'ok-'a mor

When rehearsing their dances, the men sing in low voices in a syllabic style. No instrumental accompaniment is used and the men practise in monophony, or (near) unison. In the rehearsal recorded, they sing pitches equivalent to F, A♭, B♭ and C. Phrases end on any of these pitches except A♭, which is quite rarely used. The whole verse ends on B♭. However, during performance the same words are sung at a higher pitch, transforming the melody and possibly the mode quite considerably.

The whole song consists of many verses, each of which is assembled from a series of three basic phrases. A single verse has been transcribed. Each phrase appears in two or three different forms but consists mainly of groups of repeated notes of the same pitch. Phrases labelled **A** in the transcription cadence to F, those labelled **B** are shorter and repeat the note C only, and those labelled **C** are the longest phrases with the most varied contour, cadencing to B♭. Marking variant phrases with a dash, the overall structure of the verse is **A, A', B, B', C, B, B', C', A", A', B, B', C"**.

The song does not readily fit a single Western time-signature. However, a regular beat (equivalent to a dotted crotchet in the transcription) is maintained throughout. Most often this is divided into three equal notes or two notes: one long and one short or one short and one long. Some beats are not subdivided, others are divided into two equal notes, and some long notes are sustained for two beats. Whatever the case, there is considerable rhythmic variety, nearly every new pattern contrasting with the one which preceded it.

Glossary

Brief descriptions of the main musical instruments, ensembles and terms discussed in this book are given below. More complete definitions of the Western musical terms listed here will be found in a good music dictionary. In the case of instruments and non-Western or less usual terms, reference is given to sections of the book where these are dealt with in more detail.

arghūl	Egyptian double clarinet – $^1/25$
aruding	Palawan (Philippines) jaw's harp – $^1/15$
biwa	Japanese four-stringed lute – $^1/1$
chirimía	Colombian Andean Indian flute or instrumental ensemble – $^2/27$
cimpoi	Romanian rural bagpipe – $^2/15$
codetta	phrase or short passage which rounds off a longer section
dan tranh	Vietnamese sixteen-stringed zither – $^1/9$
darabukka	Egyptian and Middle Eastern pottery goblet drum – $^1/26$
dastgāh	organizational system, mode and musical structure of Persian art music – $^1/22$
diphonic singing	the production by a vocalist of two pitches at once, often a low drone to accompany a higher overtone melody – $^1/8$
dizi (*or* **di**)	Chinese bamboo transverse flute – $^1/5$
dominant	fifth degree of a scale or mode (or pitch a fifth above the tonic in a 'gapped' scale)
ethnomusicology	the study of music from around the world, often involving a comparative approach (see also musicology)
fundamental	most basic pitch of a scale, mode or series of overtones. See also tonic
gamelan	Indonesian ensemble, generally consisting largely of gongs and other percussion – $^1/12$, $^1/13$
ghayta	Algerian wooden oboe – $^1/28$
hardingfele	Norwegian violin with four or five sympathetic strings – $^2/20$
heptatonic	'seven-note', often used to describe a scale or mode and meaning that within one octave there are seven different pitches
heterophony	a musical texture in which several musicians perform differing versions of the same melody at once
hexatonic	'six-note', often used to describe a scale or mode and meaning that within one octave there are six different pitches
hocket	technical term for the production of a composite melody or pattern from multiple interlocking voices or instruments sounded alternately – $^2/2$
inanga	eight-stringed zither from Burundi – $^2/5$
ingoma	royal drum ensemble from Burundi – $^2/6$

k'amancha	Armenian four-stringed spike fiddle – [2/11]
khāēn	Laotian mouth organ – [1/11]
kōmun'go	Korean six-stringed zither – [1/3]
maqām (*pl.* maqāmāt)	'mode', Arabic term referring to a set of notes and associated compositional guidelines – [1/23], [1/25]
masenqo	Ethiopian one-stringed spike fiddle – [2/1]
musicology	'the study of music', usually meaning the study of the art music of the West in terms of itself
nāgasvaram	South Indian oboe (or ensemble led by that instrument) – [1/20]
nawba	'suite', extended form in Moroccan art music – [1/27]
ney	Middle Eastern end-blown flute – [1/23]
ostinato	rhythmic or melodic pattern repeated as the basis of a musical performance
pentatonic	'five-note', often used to describe a scale or mode and meaning that within one octave there are five different pitches
qin	Chinese seven-stringed zither – [1/4]
rāga	'mode', 'melody' and/or 'composition', Indian term referring to a set of pitches, habitual ways of moving between them and the performances created thereby – [1/19]
sanza	lamellaphone from the Central African Republic – [2/3]
shakuhachi	Japanese bamboo end-blown flute – [1/2]
sizhu	'silk and bamboo', Chinese instrumental ensemble – [1/5]
tablature	notation for instrumental music which uses symbols to show finger positions and sometimes performance technique rather than pitches
tāla	Indian term for metrical cycle or unit – [1/20], [1/21]
taqsīm	'division', Arabic term for an improvisatory passage, prelude or piece – [1/23], [1/25]
timbila (*sing.* mbila)	Chopi (Mozambique) xylophone orchestra – [2/8]
tonic	principal note of a scale or mode when arranged in its most basic theoretical form (usually one octave ascending)
vīnā	South Indian long-necked lute – [1/19]
vioara	Romanian violin – [2/14]
vocables	'meaningless' syllables sung as part of a song – [1/6], [1/10], [2/22], [2/23]

Index of Musical Instruments

accordion 70, 78

bagpipe 79–80, 81
bell 19, 41, 55, 100

clappers 15, 16, 17, 36, 37, 61, 85
clarinet 47–48, 81–82, 101
cymbal 17, 18, 19, 29

double bass 78–79
drum 8, 12, 17, 18, 19, 27–28, 30, 36, 38, 39,
    40–41, 43, 44, 45, 48–50, 51, 53, 65–66, 69,
    81, 93, 96, 97, 99, 100, 101
dulcimer 15, 16, 43, 72, 78

fiddle 15, 16, 22, 27, 28, 43, 48–50, 51, 57–58, 59,
    72, 73–74, 78, 81, 82–84, 89–91
flute: end-blown 9–10, 15, 27, 28, 30, 43, 44–45;
    transverse, 8, 9, 15, 16, 48–50, 96, 101, 103

gong 8, 17, 27–29, 30
guitar 85–86, 87–88, 97–98, 101

harmonium 39, 41
harp-lute 55
horn 103
human body (clapping, stamping, etc.) 36, 58, 59,
    62, 69, 85–86

jaw's harp 30, 31–32

lamellaphone 60–61, 62

lute 8, 9, 10, 15, 16, 22, 30, 37–39, 41, 43, 51, 72,
    78, 81, 82–83, 82–87. *See also* guitar

mouth organ 8, 9, 15, 25–26
musical bow 67–68, 96

oboe 8, 17, 18, 19, 39–40, 53

panpipes 33–34, 70, 78, 102–103

rasp 101
rattle 61, 62, 67, 69, 96, 101, 103

shaker 100. *See also* rattle
sound-tube 33, 36–37
steel pan 99–100

tambourine 51, 81
trumpet 18

voice 16–18, 18–19, 20–21, 22, 23–24, 25, 27, 28,
    30–31, 33, 34–35, 36–37, 40, 41, 43, 45–46, 48,
    49–50, 51, 54–56, 57–58, 58–59, 60–61, 62–63,
    64–65, 65–66, 66–68, 68, 69, 70–71, 72–73,
    75–76, 76–77, 78–79, 85–86, 87–88, 91–92, 93–94,
    94–95, 96–97, 97–98, 102, 103–104

whistle 33, 69, 96

xylophone 27, 29, 55, 68–69

zither 8, 10, 11–12, 13–15, 22–23, 30, 64–65, 72

General Index